100% NEW

DEVELOPING MATHEMATICS

**Customisable
teaching resources
for mathematics**

UNDERSTANDING SHAPES AND MEASURES

Ages 8–9

**Hilary Koll and
Steve Mills**

D1102668

A & C Black • London

Contents

Understanding shape

Draw polygons and classify them by identifying their properties, including their line symmetry. Visualise 3-D objects from 2-D drawings and make nets of common solids

Recognise horizontal and vertical lines; use the eight compass points to describe direction; describe and identify the position of a square on a grid of squares

Know that angles are measured in degrees and that one whole turn is 360°; compare and order angles less than 180°

Measuring

Choose and use standard metric units and their abbreviations when estimating, measuring and recording length, weight and capacity; know the meaning of kilo, centi and milli and, where appropriate, use decimal notation to record measurements

CR
5/6
15
UND

Interpret intervals and divisions on partially numbered scales and record readings accurately, where appropriate to the nearest tenth of a unit

Draw rectangles and measure and calculate their perimeters; find the area of rectilinear shapes drawn on a square grid by counting squares

Read time to the nearest minute; use am, pm and 12-hour clock notation; choose units of time to measure time intervals; calculate time intervals from clocks and timetables

Published 2008 by A & C Black Publishers Limited
36 Soho Square, London W1D 3QY
www.acblack.com

ISBN 978-1-4081-0056-1

Copyright text © Hilary Koll and Steve Mills 2008
Copyright illustrations © Andy Robb 2008
Copyright cover illustration © Jan McCafferty 2008
Editors: Lynne Williamson and Marie Lister
Designed by Billin Design Solutions Ltd

The authors and publishers would like to thank
Catherine Yemm and Judith Wells for their advice
in producing this series of books.

A CIP catalogue record for this book is available from the British Library.

Printed and bound in Great Britain by Halstan Printing Group, Amersham, Buckinghamshire.

A & C Black uses paper produced with elemental chlorine-free pulp, harvested from managed sustainable forests.

Introduction

100% New Developing Mathematics: Understanding Shapes and Measures is a series of seven photocopiable activity books for children aged 4 to 11, designed to be used during the daily maths lesson. The books focus on the skills and concepts for Understanding Shape and Measuring as outlined in the National Strategy's *Primary Framework for literacy and mathematics*. The activities are intended to be used in the time allocated to pupil activities; they aim to reinforce the knowledge and develop the facts, skills and understanding explored during the main part of the lesson, and to provide practice and consolidation of the objectives contained in the Framework document.

Understanding Shape

This strand of the *Primary Framework for mathematics* is concerned with helping pupils to develop awareness and understanding of the properties of shapes, spatial concepts, and ideas of position and location. It covers the properties of 2-D and 3-D shapes, including angles and symmetries, together with ways of describing positions in grids, such as using coordinates.

Measuring

The 'Measuring' strand, which is also addressed in this book, includes the main measurement topics such as length, mass and capacity, together with ideas of time, area and perimeter. These topics cover estimating, comparing and measuring, including using standard metric units and converting between them.

Understanding Shapes and Measures Ages 8–9

supports the teaching of mathematics by providing a series of activities to develop spatial vocabulary in order to increase awareness of properties of shape and measurement concepts. The following learning objectives are covered:

- draw polygons and classify them by identifying their properties, including their line symmetry;
- visualise 3-D objects from 2-D drawings and make nets of common solids;
- recognise horizontal and vertical lines; use the eight compass points to describe direction; describe and identify the position of a square on a grid of squares;
- know that angles are measured in degrees and that one whole turn is 360°; compare and order angles less than 180°;
- choose and use standard metric units and their abbreviations when estimating, measuring and recording length, weight and capacity; know the meaning of kilo, centi and milli and, where appropriate,

use decimal notation to record measurements, for example 1.3 m or 0.6 kg;

- interpret intervals and divisions on partially numbered scales and record readings accurately, where appropriate to the nearest tenth of a unit;
- draw rectangles and measure and calculate their perimeters; find the area of rectilinear shapes drawn on a square grid by counting squares;
- read time to the nearest minute; use am, pm and 12-hour clock notation; choose units of time to measure time intervals; calculate time intervals from clocks and timetables.

Extension

Many of the activity sheets end with a challenge (**Now try this!**) which reinforces and extends children's learning, and provides the teacher with an opportunity for assessment. These might include harder questions, with numbers from a higher range, than those in the main part of the activity sheet. Some challenges are open-ended questions and provide opportunity for children to think mathematically for themselves. Occasionally the challenge will require additional paper or that the children write on the reverse of the sheet itself. Many of the activities encourage children to generate their own questions or puzzles for a partner to solve.

Organisation

Very little equipment is needed, but it will be useful to have available: rulers, scissors, coloured pencils, dice, counters, glue, transparent tape, small mirrors, interlocking cubes, solid shapes and squared paper. You also need to provide clocks with movable, geared hands for pages 58–61.

The children should also have access to measuring equipment to give them practical experience of length, mass and capacity.

Where possible, children's work should be supported by ICT equipment, such as number lines and tracks on interactive whiteboards, or computer software for comparing numbers and measures. It is also vital that children's experiences are introduced in real-life contexts and through

practical activities. The teachers' notes at the foot of each page and the more detailed notes on pages 6 to 11 suggest ways in which this can be done effectively.

To help teachers select appropriate learning experiences for the children, the activities are grouped into sections within the book. However, the activities are not expected to be used in this order unless stated otherwise. The sheets are intended to support, rather than direct, the teacher's planning.

Some activities can be made easier or more challenging by masking or substituting numbers. You may wish to re-use pages by copying them onto card and laminating them.

Accompanying CD

The enclosed CD-ROM contains electronic versions of the activity sheets in the book for printing, editing, saving or display on an interactive whiteboard. This means that modifications can be made to further differentiate the activities to suit individual pupils' needs. See page 12 for further details.

Teachers' notes

Brief notes are provided at the foot of each page, giving ideas and suggestions for maximising the effectiveness of the activity sheets. These can be masked before copying.

Further explanations of the activities can be found on pages 6 to 11, together with examples of questions you can ask.

Whole-class warm-up activities

The tools provided in A & C Black's Maths Skills and Practice CD-ROMs can be used as introductory activities for use with the whole class. In the Maths Skills and Practice CD-ROM 4 (ISBN 9780713673203) the following activities and games could be used to introduce or reinforce 'Shapes and Measures' objectives:

- *Area lab*
- *Build a dude*
- *Gotcha measure*
- *Pattern magic*
- *Talking time*
- *Position*

The following activities provide some practical ideas which can be used to introduce or reinforce the main teaching part of the lesson, or to provide an interesting basis for discussion.

Understanding shape
Twenty questions

Hide a 3-D shape in a bag and ask the children to find out which shape it is by asking questions. You can only answer 'yes' or 'no' to their

questions. Challenge the children to guess the shape in twenty questions.

Make a kilogram

Call out masses in grams that are less than a kilogram, for example 450 g, 992 g, 860 g, and ask the children to give the mass that would make this measurement up to 1 kilogram: 550 g, 8 g, 140 g. The same activity can be tried with measurements given in millilitres to make 1 litre.

Measuring
Number lines

Show a line split into ten sections and explain to the children that this line represents 1 km. Mark 1 km and 1000 m at one end. Count along together in tenths of a kilometre and in steps of one hundred metres. Draw a

mark at any position along the line and ask the children to say or estimate how many metres the position represents, for example: *This position represents four-tenths of a kilometre which is the same as 400 m.*

Time moves on

In the same way that children sitting in a circle might say numbers in a sequence, for example *2, 4, 6, 8...*, they can say time sequences that involve counting on or back in steps of an hour, half an hour, a quarter of an hour, or in 10- or 5-minutes

intervals, for example: *Twenty past 11, half past 11, twenty to 12, ten to 12...* Hold up a clock to show the times and discuss different ways of saying the same time, for example 'twenty to 12' or '11:40'.

Notes on the activities

Understanding shape

Draw polygons and classify them by identifying their properties, including their line symmetry. Visualise 3-D objects from 2-D drawings and make nets of common solids

It is important that children are given opportunities to work practically with 2-D and 3-D shapes, in order to develop a broad understanding of their nature and properties. The following activities can supplement these practical tasks and provide contexts and stimuli that can be more fully explored in the classroom. Encourage children to develop vocabulary skills by ensuring that activities are undertaken in pairs or small groups and that whole-class discussions take place frequently. Children should know the meaning of faces, vertices and edges of 3-D shapes and should become familiar with reflective symmetries of 2-D shapes. Nets of 3-D shapes should also be explored at this age.

Proper properties game and Shapes: 1 and 2
(pages 13–15)

Discuss the properties on the property cards and ensure that the children are familiar with the terms 'vertical' and 'horizontal'. The cards on Shapes: 1 and 2 can be used for other activities, such as picking a card and writing a detailed description of it including, where appropriate, the coordinates of the vertices, or describing one of the shapes to a partner for them to guess which shape it is.

SUGGESTED QUESTIONS:

- How many sides/corners/angles does this shape have?
- Does this shape have a line of symmetry?
- Is it vertical or horizontal?

Brooches (page 16)

Encourage the children to use small mirrors to test their answers. Perspex equipment (such as a MIRA) that allows not only the reflection to be seen but also the drawing on the other side of the line can be a useful resource for those children who struggle with mirrors. Discuss any lines drawn incorrectly.

SUGGESTED QUESTIONS:

- Is this brooch symmetrical?
- How many lines of symmetry does this brooch have?

Decorations (page 17)

This activity revises the shape names and encourages the children to realise that pentagons and hexagons can take many forms.

At the start of the lesson, demonstrate how a two-criteria intersecting Venn diagram is used to sort data. Discuss the intersection and remind the children that numbers can be written outside the circle (inside the rectangle) to represent items that do not meet either of the criteria given.

SUGGESTED QUESTIONS:

- Do you know what a four-sided shape is called?
- How many sides/vertices/angles has this shape?

The great shape game (page 18)

Playing the game outlined in the teachers' notes at the foot of the page encourages the children to visualise and make different 2-D shapes and explore the properties. It is possible to make many different grey shapes with the cards. Here is an example of the shapes that have been made from all the cards at the end of one game:

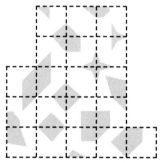

The children could score bonus points for saying the number of right angles that a completed shape has. The children could also work individually to try to put different cards together to make three squares. As an alternative individual activity, the children could try to make as many different symmetrical shapes as they can.

SUGGESTED QUESTIONS:

- Do you know the name of this shape?
- How many sides/right angles/lines of symmetry has this shape?

Party presents (page 19)

Ensure that the children know the terms 'faces', 'vertices' and 'edges', and know that 'vertex' is the singular of 'vertices'.

SUGGESTED QUESTIONS:

- What shapes are the faces of a cube/cuboid/triangular prism?
- Which shapes have one or more curved faces?

Cube challenge (page 20)

The children can be asked to make a further range of shapes with the four models and to sketch the shapes made. Please note that there is more than one way to make the fourth shape (see Answers on page 63).

SUGGESTED QUESTIONS:

- How many cubes have you used to make this shape?
- Can you colour the picture to match the colour of your cubes?

Nets with pentagons/triangles/rectangles/circles
(pages 21–24)

It is important that children have experience in making their own nets and joining them together to form 3-D shapes. These four worksheets provide templates for making different types of 3-D shapes, including pyramids, prisms, cuboids, a cone and a cylinder. Once the children have made the shapes they could go on to explore different nets that could be used to make the same shapes, for example where the faces are arranged in different positions to make the same shape.

SUGGESTED QUESTIONS:

• What shape do you think this one will make?
• How many faces has this shape?
• How do you think it will fit together?

Crazy cubes (page 25)

As the children begin to appreciate what a net is they can begin to explore patterns on different faces. Some children will find this visualisation very difficult, whereas other, more spatially aware, children may find this easier. Children who struggle need to be given situations where they can explore the nets practically by cutting out and folding the nets to see what happens to the shape.

SUGGESTED PROMPT/QUESTIONS:

• Look at the net. How many faces have squares on?
• What does this tell you about this cube?
• Are the 'L' shapes all in a straight line?

Recognise horizontal and vertical lines; use the eight compass points to describe direction; describe and identify the position of a square on a grid of squares

> Children should develop an understanding of a range of positional, directional and distance words and be able to use them to interpret and give their own instructions. Instructions should contain: position, such as locating a square in a grid; direction, such as left and right or using the eight compass points; and movement, indicating the distance of the movement (for example 3 squares, or 4 units).

Optical illusions (page 26)

These common optical illusions can be discussed and then the children encouraged to colour the horizontal lines blue ('think of the horizon over the sea') and the vertical lines red ('think of a tall red tower').

SUGGESTED QUESTION:

• Is the line vertical or horizontal?

Pirates of the Pacific (page 27)

At the start of the lesson, ask the children to stand and face the direction that you tell them is North. Revise South, East, West and North, and then talk about the points of the compass that come between each of them.

SUGGESTED QUESTIONS:

• In which direction would you travel from here to here?
• Is this East or West?
• Which direction is North-West?

Zap 'em: 1 and 2 (pages 28 – 29)

It is important that children remember which colour their own counters are and that they understand that they have to try to remove the other player's coloured counters from the game board.

SUGGESTED QUESTIONS:

• In which direction would you travel from here to here?
• Which card do you need in order to win the game?

Counter attack (page 30)

This activity involves direction, using the eight compass points, and distance. It can help children to appreciate that there are opposite directions, for example one square NE followed by one square SW returns you to the same position. Encourage the children who complete the extension activity to use as many different directions as they can in their puzzles.

SUGGESTED QUESTIONS:

• Can you follow this set of instructions?
• Where would you end up?

Cinema seating (page 31)

This activity provides practice in identifying squares on a grid using letters and numbers. The descriptions on the worksheet can be altered to provide further practice and variety.

SUGGESTED QUESTION:

• Which seats are either side of D3?

Know that angles are measured in degrees and that one whole turn is 360°; compare and order angles less than 180°

> The basis of all angle work is the idea of turning. Many children have struggled with the ideas of angle because they have been given insufficient time to appreciate turn and have moved too quickly on to static angles, causing misconceptions that the angle between two lines is related to line length, area inside the arc, distance between the two end-points of the lines, and not related to the amount of turn that would take one line onto the other.
>
> Therefore, it is very important that children explore turning practically before they begin to explore angles in static pictures and shapes. They should recognise and make whole, half and quarter turns as a precursor for understanding and recognising the nature of angles. At this age children should be beginning to understand that angles are measured in degrees, and that there are 360° in a full turn (four 90° right angles).

Hickory, dickory, dock (page 32)

This first angle activity encourages the children to see patterns in the sizes of angles on a clock. They should notice that the number of degrees goes up in thirties and that a right angle is 90°, a straight angle is 180° and a full turn is 360°.

- Which clock shows a right angle?
- How many degrees in a full turn/a half turn?

Angelina's angles (page 33)

It is useful if children have had experience of making turning angles using a piece of knotted wool through a hole in a circle. It can help them appreciate that angle is about turning, rather than only seeing angles as static representations. Once the children are aware that there are 90° in a right angle and 360° in a full turn they can begin to estimate the sizes of angles.

SUGGESTED QUESTIONS:

- About how many degrees do you think this angle is?
- Is this angle larger or smaller than a right angle?
- How can you check?

Safe-breaker (page 34)

The instructions on this worksheet can be altered to provide more variety and differentiation.

SUGGESTED QUESTIONS:

- Can you follow another group's instructions?
- Where would the arrow end up?

Magic spell (page 35)

Introduce this activity practically by drawing a large wheel on paper or in chalk on the playground. Explain that each section of the wheel is 30°. Choose a child to stand in the centre of the wheel and ask him/her to rotate as other children give instructions.

SUGGESTED QUESTIONS:

- Can you follow your partner's instructions?
- What word do you spell?

Scissor angles (page 36)

These cards can also be used for individual comparison activities, for example the children could pick four cards and put the angles in order of size, starting with the smallest.

SUGGESTED QUESTIONS:

- Is this angle larger than this angle?
- Have the scissors here been opened further than in this picture?

Angle tangle (page 37)

Here the children are drawing their own angles which they then put in order of size, smallest to largest. Draw attention to the link between a pair of scissors and the angles they have drawn, for example by encouraging them to think of their lines as scissor blades. Some children may need to trace the angles and place them on top of each other in order to compare the sizes.

SUGGESTED QUESTIONS:

- Is this angle larger than this angle?
- If these were pictures of scissors, have these blades been opened further than the ones in this picture?

That's an order! (page 38)

In the final activity in this series of worksheets, the children are given static angles to order. Again, make the link between the sizes of the angles and scissor blades to encourage the children to appreciate the amount of turn. Some children may need to trace the angles and place them on top of each other in order to compare the sizes.

SUGGESTED QUESTIONS:

- Is this angle larger than this angle?
- If these were pictures of scissors, have these blades been opened further than the ones in this picture?

Measuring

Choose and use standard metric units and their abbreviations when estimating, measuring and recording length, weight and capacity; know the meaning of kilo, centi and milli and, where appropriate, use decimal notation to record measurements, for example 1.3 m or 0.6 kg

Children of this age are beginning to become familiar with centimetres, metres, kilometres, grams, kilograms, millilitres and litres. They should know the abbreviations of these and the relationships between the main standard units of length, mass and capacity, and begin to be able to use them when estimating, measuring, reading and recording measurements.

It is vital that children are given as much practical experience as possible in order that they gain a full appreciation of the units, in particular those of mass and capacity, to enable them to estimate and check that measurements are sensible.

Measure for measure (page 39)

This practical activity is best done in pairs or in small groups as it encourages discussion and requires fewer pieces of measuring equipment. If the children are not using electronic scales to measure the mass of the shoe and the trainer then the degree of accuracy will need to be changed before the worksheet is given to the children.

Begin the lesson by discussing the meaning of the terms 'mass' and 'weight'.

In the extension activity, the children should realise that length and width together give an idea of size. As a further extension, they could be asked to measure other aspects of the items in order to describe them fully, for example collar size.

SUGGESTED QUESTIONS:

- What piece of measuring equipment did you use to measure the mass of the shoe?
- What unit of measurement did you use to describe the length of the sleeve of the jumper? Could you have used a different unit?
- How accurately did you measure?

Measure together (page 40)

This activity involves the children selecting the correct unit of measurement and then trying to estimate or find out the answers to each question, using appropriate instruments where possible.

At the start of the lesson, ask the children to tell you all the units of measurement that they know and list these on the board. Ask the children to link the measures together and to order them by size, for example 10 mm = 1 cm, 100 cm = 1 m, 1000 m = 1 km; mm, cm, m, km.

These cards could be enlarged and laminated to create a more permanent resource.

SUGGESTED QUESTIONS:

- How could you find the answer to this question?
- Can you estimate the answer and then measure to check?
- What piece of equipment will you use to find out the answer?

Made to measure (page 41)

At the start of the lesson, remind the children that 100 cm is the same as 1 m and discuss how far this distance is in relation to a metre stick.

SUGGESTED QUESTIONS:

- How do you know that 3.2 m is equivalent to 320 cm?
- Is a 3.5 m scarf longer or shorter than 35 cm?

Guinea pig food (page 42)

At the start of the lesson, remind the children that 1000 g is the same as 1 kg and pass round weights so that the children can begin to develop a sense of how heavy 1 kg or 1000 g is. Explain that 1 g is the weight of water that would fit into a centimetre cube (if that were possible).

SUGGESTED QUESTIONS:

- How many grams is the same as 1 kilogram?
- Can you suggest something that would weigh about 1.5 kg?

Milking Milli (page 43)

At the start of the lesson, remind the children that 1000 ml is the same as 1 litre and pass round a container, bottle or carton that holds a litre of liquid. This will help the children to begin to develop a sense of how much 1 litre or 1000 ml is. Explain that 1 ml is the amount of water that would fit into a centimetre cube (if that were possible).

SUGGESTED QUESTIONS:

- How many millilitres are there in a litre?
- Can you suggest something that would hold about 1.5 l?

Interpret intervals and divisions on partially numbered scales and record readings accurately, where appropriate to the nearest tenth of a unit

It is important that children become familiar with different types of scales on a range of measuring instruments and begin to learn how to interpret the reading. Initially, children should read from scales where all divisions are numbered and then should move on to those where the interval marks are shown but not numbered. This requires them to work out what each unnumbered mark represents. Encourage the children to count up in even-sized steps to check that the value of each interval matches the given numbers.

Fi's fruitcake (page 44)

Ensure the children appreciate that the previous ingredients remain in the pan of the scales as the new ingredient is added. As a further extension, the children could write out a list of ingredients and the amounts for a new recipe and then draw arrows on scales to show these amounts.

SUGGESTED QUESTION:

- What is each interval worth on these scales?

Fill it up! (page 45)

Explain that the aim of this game is to fill your container before your partner, adding new amounts and indicating this by colouring the new amount. Explain that at the end of each go the children should say exactly how much liquid they have in their container and also how much more or less they have than their partner.

SUGGESTED QUESTIONS:

- How much more liquid do you need to reach 1 litre?
- How much liquid have you now?

Potion pathways (page 46)

The following list explains the errors made if the children gave the answer as anything other than pot **H**.

Pot A – *two errors: children have not noticed that the weighing scales at the start are marked in kilograms; they have given 75 ml as equivalent to 3/4 of a litre (should be 750 ml).*

Pot B – *three errors: children have not noticed that the weighing scales at the start are marked in kilograms; they have given 75 ml as equivalent to 3/4 of a litre (should be 750 ml); they have read the scale on the minute timer incorrectly.*

Pot C – *one error: children have not noticed that the weighing scales at the start are marked in kilograms.*

Pot D – *t wo errors: children have not noticed that the weighing scales at the start are marked in kilograms; they have not realised that 5.5 kg is equivalent to 5500 g.*

Pot E – *three errors: children have not noticed that the weighing scales at the start are marked in kilograms; they have not recognised that 500 ml is half a litre; they have read the temperature scale incorrectly as -6° C, rather than as -4° C.*

OR

two errors: children have not recognised that 350 ml is not more than $\frac{1}{2}$ litre, they have read the temperature scale incorrectly as -6° C, rather than as -4° C.

Pot F – *one error: children have not recognised that 350 ml is not more than $\frac{1}{2}$ litre.*

Pot G – *one error: children have read the right-hand weighing scales as 152 g (should be 170 g).*

SUGGESTED QUESTIONS:

* What is three-quarters of a litre?
* What is three-quarters of a kilogram?
* How do we read this scale where the level is between numbered marks?

Speedometers (page 47)

Encourage the children to count up in even-sized steps to check that the value of each interval matches the given numbers.

SUGGESTED QUESTION:

* What is the value of each small interval?

Scale shapes (page 48)

This activity involves a wide variety of scales. Encourage the children to count up in even-sized steps to check that the value of each interval matches the given numbers. As an extension, the children can write something that is being measured for each of the scales on the worksheet, for example 30 ml could be the amount of concentrated drink put in a mug before filling with water.

SUGGESTED QUESTION:

* What do you think might be being measured here?

Draw rectangles and measure and calculate their perimeters; find the area of rectilinear shapes drawn on a square grid by counting squares

When children are introduced to perimeter and area together they can often confuse the two ideas. Begin by exploring perimeter and emphasise that the perimeter is a length, like a trail, around the outline of a shape.

When introducing area emphasise that area is the amount of space inside the shape and that it is measured in squares. The following area activities all involve squares that children can count at this stage. Moving children too quickly on to the formula for finding the area of a rectangle can often lead children to a misunderstanding of the nature of area and should be avoided at this stage.

Perimeter puzzles (page 49)

When measuring sides and finding perimeters, encourage the children to notice that opposite sides of rectangles are equal in length and that the length and the width can be added and then doubled to find the perimeter. As a further extension, ask the children to make up their own perimeter puzzles for a partner to solve.

SUGGESTED QUESTIONS:

* What is the length of this side? What do you notice about the length of the opposite side?
* How long is the perimeter of each badge?

Spot the rectangles (page 50)

Ensure that the children know the terms 'horizontal' and 'vertical', and they appreciate that for this activity the rectangles must have horizontal and vertical sides.

SUGGESTED QUESTIONS:

* What is the length of this side?
* What do you notice about the length of the opposite side?

Seeing stars (page 51)

This activity again reinforces that perimeters are lengths and can be measured in centimetres. It also encourages children to realise that it is not necessary to measure and add every side together where a shape has equal sides. Multiplication by ten can be used here.

SUGGESTED QUESTION:

* How can you draw a shape with a perimeter of 80 cm?

Area llamas (pages 52)

The children will need 1 cm² paper for the extension activity.

SUGGESTED QUESTIONS:

* How many centimetre squares are in this shape?
* What is its area?

Mosaic numbers (pages 53)

The children will need 1 cm² paper for the extension activity.

SUGGESTED QUESTIONS:

* Which numbers have the same area?
* Which number has the largest area?

Fair and square (page 54)

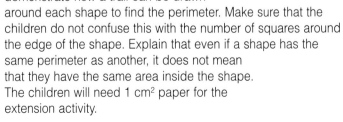

At the start of the lesson, provide the children with the worksheet and demonstrate how a trail can be drawn around each shape to find the perimeter. Make sure that the children do not confuse this with the number of squares around the edge of the shape. Explain that even if a shape has the same perimeter as another, it does not mean that they have the same area inside the shape. The children will need 1 cm² paper for the extension activity.

SUGGESTED QUESTIONS:

- What is the area of this shape?
- What is its perimeter?

Read time to the nearest minute; use am, pm and 12-hour clock notation; choose units of time to measure time intervals; calculate time intervals from clocks and timetables

Children of this age should be becoming confident with telling the time to the nearest minute on analogue clocks (those with faces) and on digital clocks, and be able to describe times in many different ways.

The children should also begin to appreciate time intervals, such as saying what time it will be in 25 minutes or in three-quarters of an hour, or saying the length of time between two given times.

Time dominoes (page 55)

Encourage the children to check each other's clocks before beginning the bingo game. The times can be altered to make them easier or harder, as appropriate.

SUGGESTED QUESTIONS:

- What time does this clock show?
- Can you find a matching clock?

Time bingo (page 56)

Encourage the children to check each other's clocks before beginning the bingo game. The times can be altered to make them easier or harder, as appropriate.

SUGGESTED QUESTIONS:

- What time does this clock show?
- Can we describe this time in a different way?

Dan's day (page 57)

At the start of the lesson, ask children what they might be doing at six o'clock. Discuss how their answers vary according to whether they think it is six o'clock in the morning or six o'clock in the evening. Show how 'am' and 'pm' are used to differentiate between morning, afternoon, evening and night. Explain that noon is 12 pm and midnight is 12 am.

SUGGESTED QUESTIONS:

- If the time had been 7:30 pm instead, which of those activities might Dan have been doing?
- What are the differences between what you might be doing at 9:00 am and at 9:00 pm?

Loopy time intervals: 1 and 2 (pages 58–59)

Loopy time intervals: 1 provides an opportunity for children to practise reading digital clock faces and to work out what the time must be before/after given time intervals. Loopy time intervals: 2 practises the reading of analogue clocks and the calculation of times. Provide analogue clocks with movable geared hands to help the children with these activities.

SUGGESTED QUESTIONS:

- What time does this clock show?
- What time would it be 2 hours later/earlier?

Poorly pets (page 60)

You can use this activity to assess the children's ability to read the time on analogue clocks as well as on digital clocks. Provide analogue clocks with movable geared hands to help the children with this activity.

SUGGESTED QUESTIONS/PROMPT:

- How did you work out that 45 minutes later than 2:21 is six minutes past three?
- The time is a quarter to three. What time did the analogue clock show 23 minutes ago?

What's the difference? (page 61)

At the start of the lesson, say a time and ask the children to say how many minutes until the next hour, for example 5:27 (33 minutes to six o'clock). Develop this to minutes just past the hour, for example 5:40 to 6:03, 5:38 to 6:05. Provide analogue clocks with movable geared hands to help the children with this activity.

SUGGESTED QUESTIONS:

- What method did you use to work out the difference between those times?
- How could you work out the difference between 3:45 and 4:51?

The number 56 bus (page 62)

At the start of the lesson, demonstrate how a timetable of this type is used and encourage the children to notice that the different buses take the same time between stops on each of the routes.

SUGGESTED QUESTIONS:

- How long does it take to get from Pyramid Shopping Centre to the Swimming Pool?
- Which bus would you get if you wanted to get to the Swimming Pool for 9:20?

Using the CD-ROM

The PC CD-ROM included with this book contains an easy-to-use software program that allows you to print out pages from the book, to view them (e.g. on an interactive whiteboard) or to customise the activities to suit the needs of your pupils.

Getting started

It's easy to run the software. Simply insert the CD-ROM into your CD drive and the disk should autorun and launch the interface in your web browser.

If the disk does not autorun, open 'My Computer' and select the CD drive, then open the file 'start.html'.

Please note: this CD-ROM is designed for use on a PC. It will also run on most Apple Macintosh computers in Safari however, due to the differences between Mac and PC fonts, you may experience some unavoidable variations in the typography and page layouts of the activity sheets.

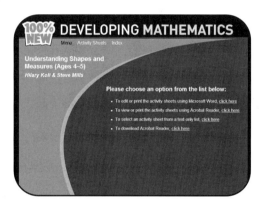

The Menu screen

Four options are available to you from the main menu screen.

The first option takes you to the Activity Sheets screen, where you can choose an activity sheet to edit or print out using Microsoft Word.

(If you do not have the Microsoft Office suite, you might like to consider using OpenOffice instead. This is a multi-platform and multi-lingual office suite, and an 'open-source' project. It is compatible with all other major office suites, and the product is free to download, use and distribute. The homepage for OpenOffice on the Internet is: www.openoffice.org.)

The second option on the main menu screen opens a PDF file of the entire book using Adobe Reader (see below). This format is ideal for printing out copies of the activity sheets or for displaying them, for example on an interactive whiteboard.

The third option allows you to choose a page to edit from a text-only list of the activity sheets, as an alternative to the graphical interface on the Activity Sheets screen.

Adobe Reader is free to download and to use. If it is not already installed on your computer, the fourth link takes you to the download page on the Adobe website.

You can also navigate directly to any of the three screens at any time by using the tabs at the top.

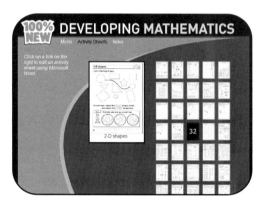

The Activity Sheets screen

This screen shows thumbnails of all the activity sheets in the book. Rolling the mouse over a thumbnail highlights the page number and also brings up a preview image of the page.

Click on the thumbnail to open a version of the page in Microsoft Word (or an equivalent software program, see above.) The full range of editing tools are available to you here to customise the page to suit the needs of your particular pupils. You can print out copies of the page or save a copy of your edited version onto your computer.

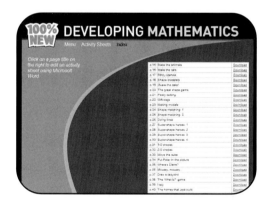

The Index screen

This is a text-only version of the Activity Sheets screen described above. Choose an activity sheet and click on the 'download' link to open a version of the page in Microsoft Word to edit or print out.

Technical support

If you have any questions regarding the *100% New Developing Literacy* or *Developing Mathematics* software, please email us at the address below. We will get back to you as quickly as possible.

educationalsales@acblack.com

Proper properties game

- **Cut out a set of property cards each.**
- **Play this game with a partner.**

You also need the cards from Shapes: 1 and 2.

☆ Put your property cards face up in front of you and the shape cards face down in a pile.

☆ Take turns to turn over a shape card and choose one of your property cards that describes the shape, if you can.

☆ Read it aloud and if your partner agrees, turn the property card face down.

☆ The winner is the first player to turn all their property cards face down.

Player one's property cards

It has exactly three right angles. **1**	It is symmetrical about a horizontal mirror line. **2**	It has four right angles. **3**	It is symmetrical about a vertical mirror line. **4**	It is a quadrilateral. **5**
All its sides are of equal length. **6**	It is a pentagon. **7**	It has eight lines of symmetry. **8**	It has two vertical sides. **9**	It is a triangle. **10**

Player two's property cards

It has exactly three right angles. **1**	It is symmetrical about a horizontal mirror line. **2**	It has four right angles. **3**	It is symmetrical about a vertical mirror line. **4**	It is a quadrilateral. **5**
All its sides are of equal length. **6**	It is a pentagon. **7**	It has eight lines of symmetry. **8**	It has two vertical sides. **9**	It is a triangle. **10**

Teachers' note Use this sheet in conjunction with pages 14 and 15, Shapes: 1 and 2. The children should cut out these cards so that they have ten property cards each. The shape cards should also be cut out (ideally having been copied onto thin card) and placed in a pile.

100% New Developing Mathematics Understanding Shapes and Measures: Ages 8–9
© A & C BLACK

Shapes: 1

• **Cut out the cards.**

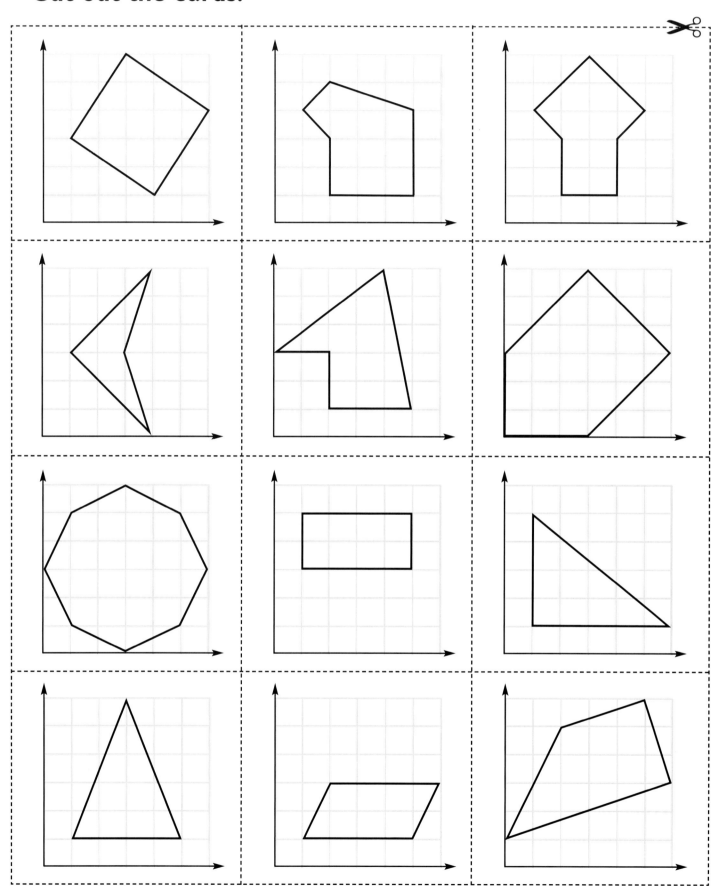

Teachers' note Use this sheet in conjunction with pages 13 and 15. Copy the sheet onto thin card and ask the children to cut out the cards. The cards could be laminated to provide a more permanent classroom resource. Explain that the arrows on the shape cards show the horizontal and vertical directions.

100% New Developing Mathematics Understanding Shapes and Measures: Ages 8–9 © A & C BLACK

Shapes: 2

• **Cut out the cards.**

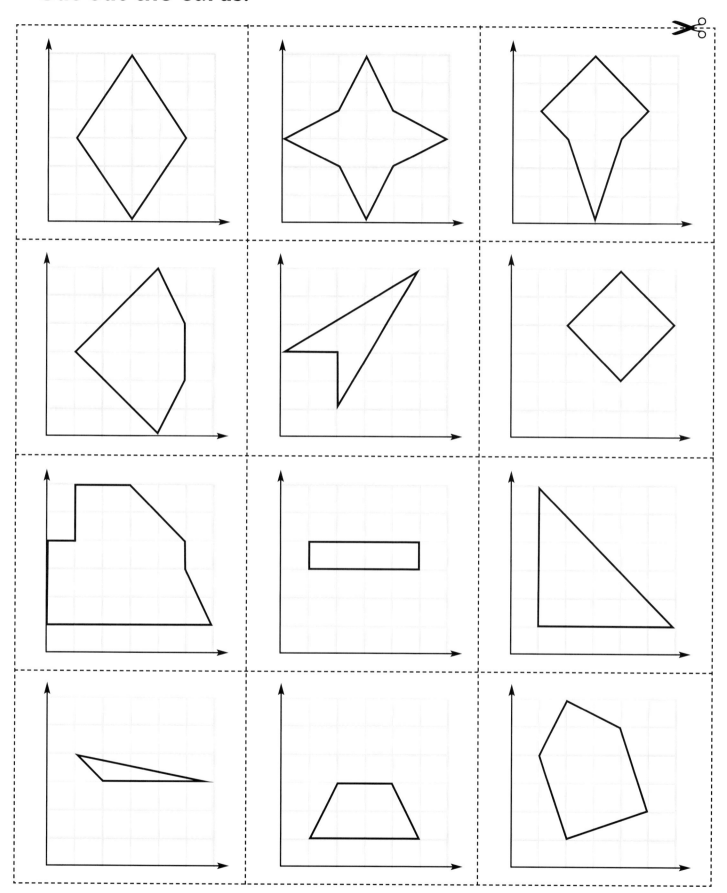

Teachers' note Use this sheet in conjunction with pages 13 and 14. Copy the sheet onto thin card and ask the children to cut out the cards. The cards could be laminated to provide a more permanent classroom resource. Explain that the arrows on the shape cards show the horizontal and vertical directions.

100% New Developing Mathematics Understanding Shapes and Measures: Ages 8–9
© A & C BLACK

Brooches

- **Draw all the lines of symmetry on each brooch. Some are <u>not</u> symmetrical.**

One has been done for you.

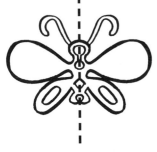  

NOW TRY THIS!

- **Design your own brooch with three or six lines of symmetry.**

Teachers' note Some of these brooches have rotational but not reflective symmetry. Watch out for children who may mistakenly think that lines of symmetry can be drawn on such brooches. Demonstrate where shapes are not symmetrical by tracing or cutting out the brooch and showing how the halves do not match when folded.

100% New Developing Mathematics Understanding Shapes and Measures: Ages 8–9 © A & C BLACK

Decorations

Here are some festival decorations.

- **Use this key to colour them.**

Key

triangles	blue
quadrilaterals	red
pentagons	yellow
hexagons	green

a 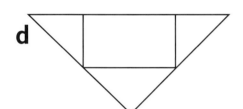   **b** 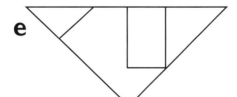   **c**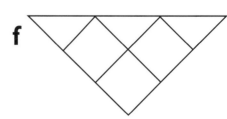

d 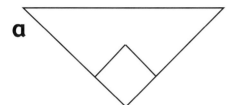   **e** 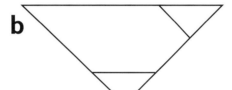   **f**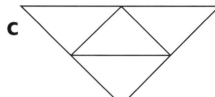

g    **h** 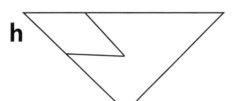   **i**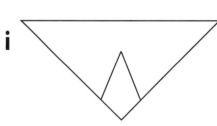

NOW TRY THIS!

- **Write the matching letter in the correct section of the** [Venn diagram] .

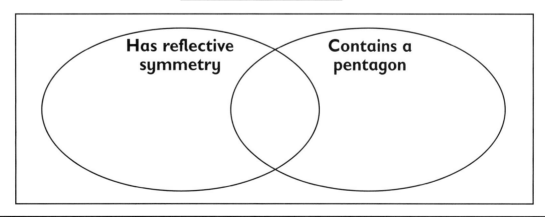

Has reflective symmetry

Contains a pentagon

Teachers' note As a further extension, the children could draw and complete another Venn diagram and label it 'Is not symmetrical' and 'Has vertical sides'.

100% New Developing Mathematics
Understanding Shapes and
Measures: Ages 8–9
© A & C BLACK

17

The great shape game

- ## This is a game for 2 or 4 players.

Teachers' note The children cut out the cards and share them out. The first player puts down a card, chooses a grey shape and names it. The number of sides equals the number of points scored. The next player then places a card alongside it (with a whole side touching) to make a new grey shape. The winner is the player with the most points when all the cards have been placed.

100% New Developing Mathematics Understanding Shapes and Measures: Ages 8–9 © A & C BLACK

Party presents

• **Colour the presents that are** | prisms | .

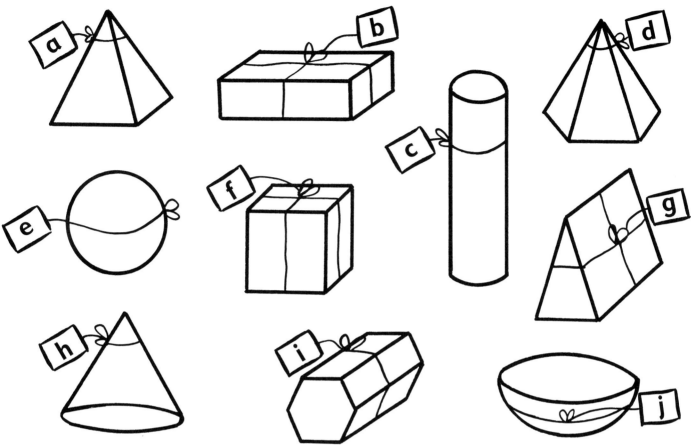

NOW TRY THIS!

• **Write which present each child brought.**

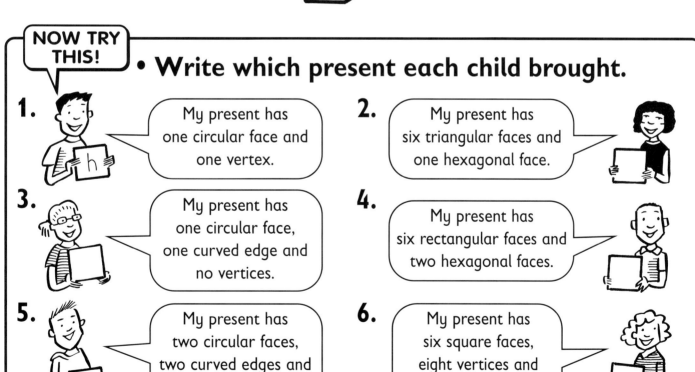

1. My present has one circular face and one vertex.

2. My present has six triangular faces and one hexagonal face.

3. My present has one circular face, one curved edge and no vertices.

4. My present has six rectangular faces and two hexagonal faces.

5. My present has two circular faces, two curved edges and no vertices.

6. My present has six square faces, eight vertices and twelve edges.

Teachers' note Remind the children that prisms have the same cross-section throughout their length. Provide the children with matching solid shapes to enable them to count and examine the properties. As a further extension, the children could write descriptions of the other shapes, referring to faces, edges and vertices.

100% New Developing Mathematics Understanding Shapes and Measures: Ages 8–9 © A & C BLACK

19

Cube challenge

- ## Make each shape in the colours shown.

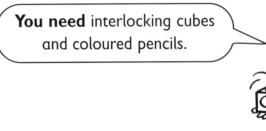

You need interlocking cubes and coloured pencils.

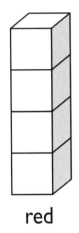
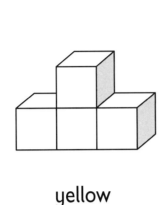
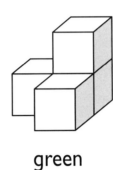

red   yellow   green   blue

- ## Now make each model below using two of your shapes.
- ## Colour the faces of each picture to show how you did it.

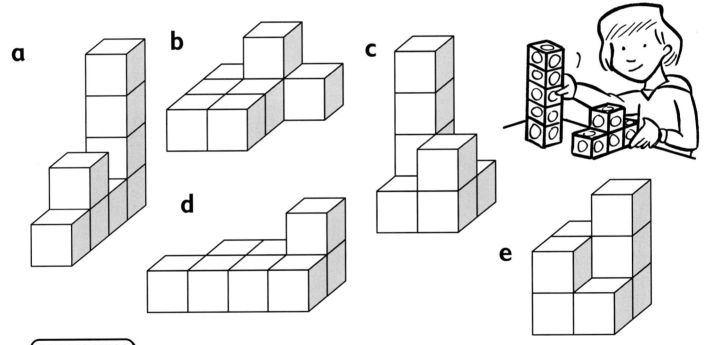

a   b   c   d   e

NOW TRY THIS!

- ## Build this cuboid using all four of your shapes.
- ## Colour the faces to show how you did it.

Teachers' note Ensure that the children have a range of coloured Multilink cubes to make these shapes and the appropriate coloured pencils. As a further extension, the children could make a model using two of the shapes and try to draw a picture of it.

100% New Developing Mathematics Understanding Shapes and Measures: Ages 8–9
© A & C BLACK

Nets with pentagons

- **Cut out the** nets .
- **Fold along the lines to make** 3-D **shapes.**

You need scissors, glue and sticky tape.

tab

tab

tab

tab

tab

tab

tab

tab

tab

tab

tab

tab

tab

tab

tab

tab

Teachers' note Copy this worksheet onto thin card, or glue the sheet onto thicker card. Once constructed, the shapes could be coloured so that no two touching faces are the same colour.

100% New Developing Mathematics Understanding Shapes and Measures: Ages 8–9
© A & C BLACK

Nets with triangles

- **Cut out the** nets .
- **Fold along the lines to make** 3-D **shapes.**

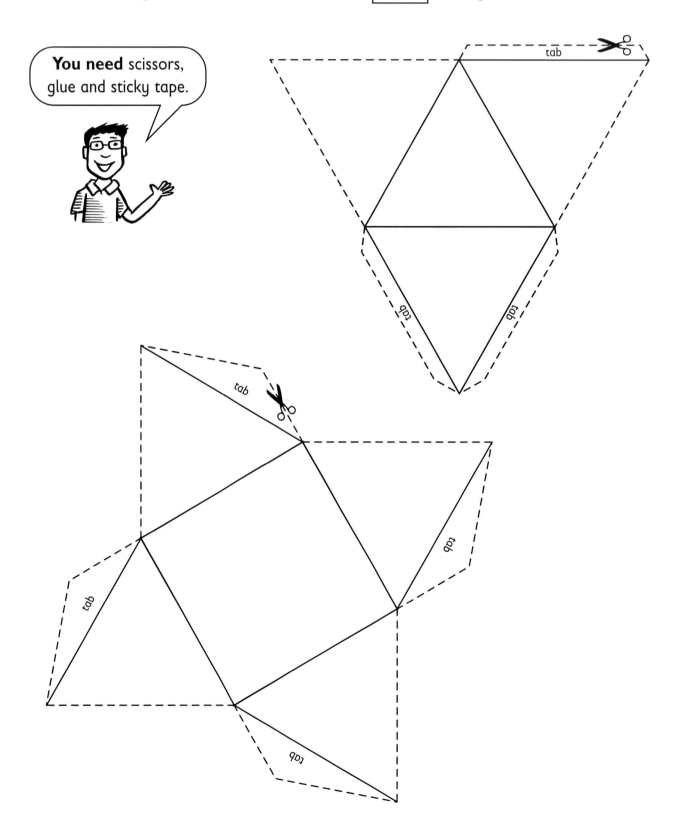

Teachers' note Copy this worksheet onto thin card, or glue the sheet onto thicker card. Once constructed, the shapes could be coloured so that no two touching faces are the same colour.

100% New Developing Mathematics Understanding Shapes and Measures: Ages 8–9
© A & C BLACK

Nets with rectangles

- **Cut out the** nets .
- **Fold along the lines to make** 3-D **shapes.**

You need scissors, glue and sticky tape.

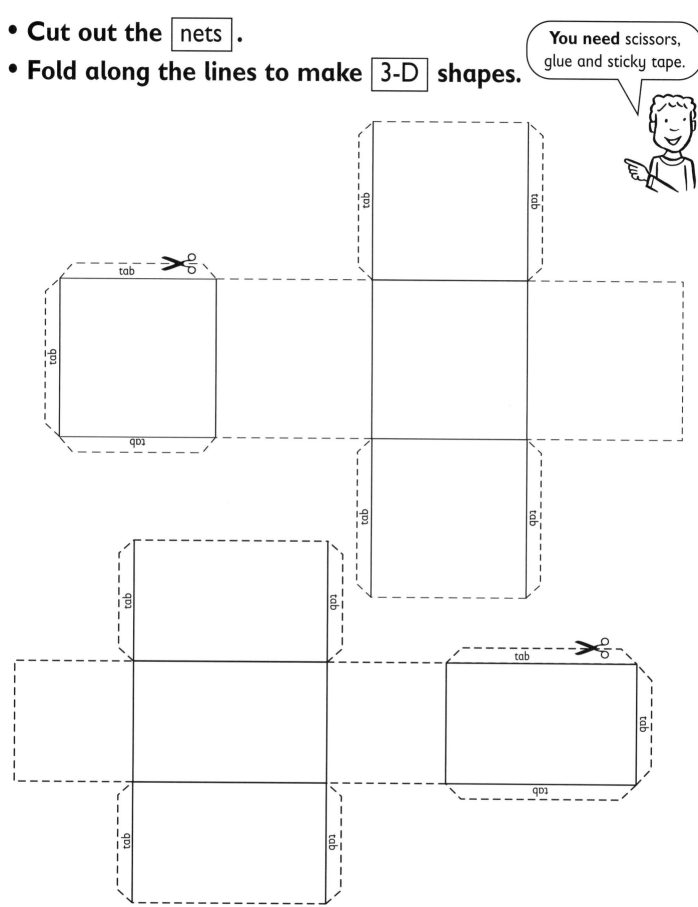

Teachers' note Copy this worksheet onto thin card, or glue the sheet onto thicker card. Once constructed, the shapes could be coloured so that no two touching faces are the same colour.

100% New Developing Mathematics Understanding Shapes and Measures: Ages 8–9 © A & C BLACK

23

- **Cut out the** nets .
- **Fold along the lines to make** 3-D **shapes.**

You need scissors, glue and sticky tape.

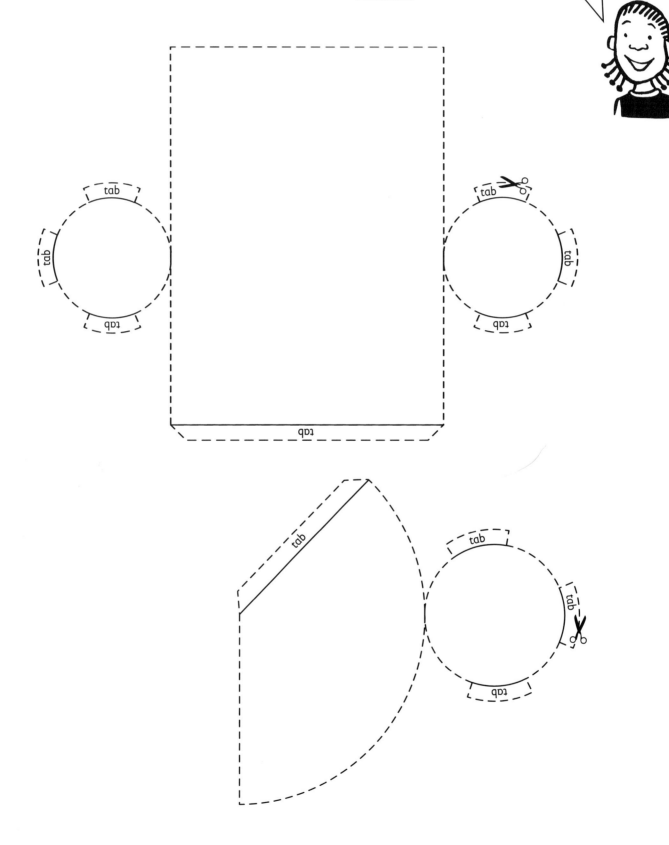

Teachers' note Copy this worksheet onto thin card, or glue the sheet onto thicker card. Be prepared to help children who accidentally cut off the circles from the main net.

100% New Developing Mathematics Understanding Shapes and Measures: Ages 8–9
© A & C BLACK

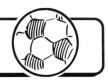

Crazy cubes

• Tick the cube that you think matches each net.

1.

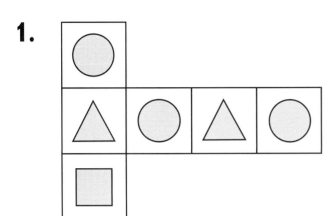

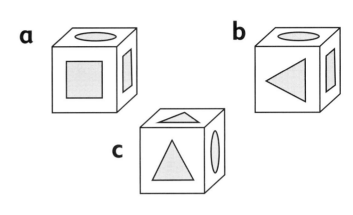

a   b   c

2.

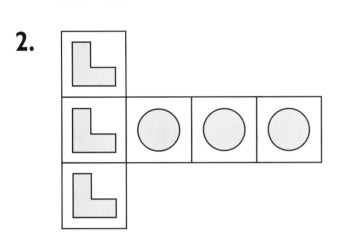

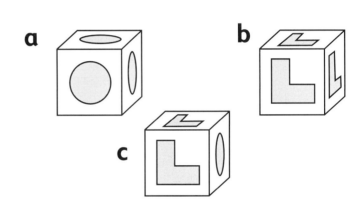

a   b   c

3.

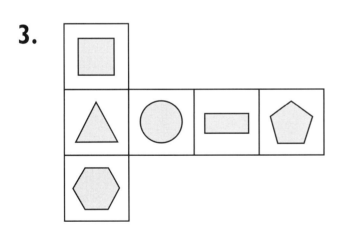

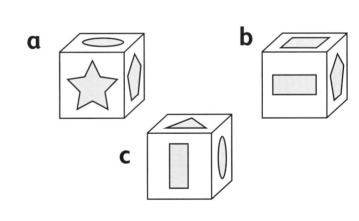

a   b   c

• Now cut out the nets to check your answers.

NOW TRY THIS!

• Make your own cube net with shapes on it.
• ⬚Sketch⬚ the cube from different angles.

Teachers' note Some children may find it difficult to visualise the cubes from the nets and will need to make up each cube and match it to a picture. The children could use sticky tape to hold the faces of the cubes together. The sheet could be enlarged to A3 size and stuck onto card to make the nets more permanent.

100% New Developing Mathematics
Understanding Shapes and
Measures: Ages 8–9
© A & C BLACK

Optical illusions

Look carefully at these designs.
- **Colour** horizontal **lines blue.**
- **Colour** vertical **lines red.**

Not every design has both **horizontal** and **vertical** lines. Use a ruler to help you check.

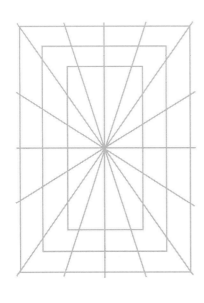

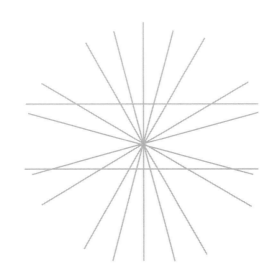

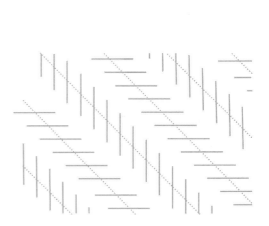

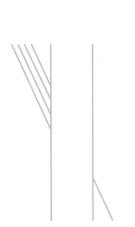

NOW TRY THIS!

- **Now try this design.**

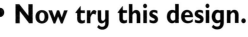

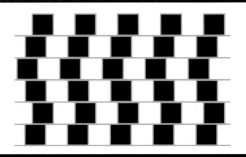

Teachers' note Optical illusions are an interesting way to introduce discussion about the terms 'vertical' and 'horizontal'. Explain that sometimes your eyes deceive you when looking at patterns and lines that look wavy can sometimes be straight. Encourage the use of rulers to check the direction and straightness of the different lines.

100% New Developing Mathematics Understanding Shapes and Measures: Ages 8–9
© A & C BLACK

Pirates of the Pacific

A board game has ships marked and labelled with letters.

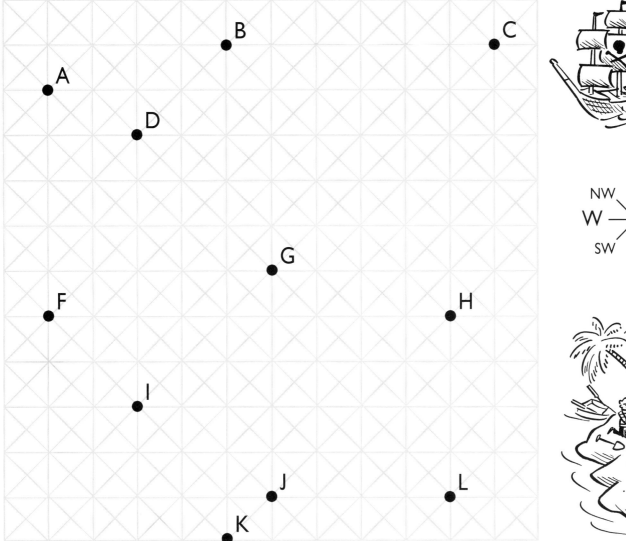

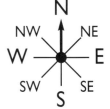

- **Use the eight points of the compass to say in which direction you must sail to go from:**

1. A to L _SE_ **2.** F to H ____ **3.** B to K ____ **4.** G to I ____

5. I to D ____ **6.** H to J ____ **7.** L to H ____ **8.** B to D ____

9. C to B ____ **10.** G to C ____ **11.** A to F ____ **12.** G to D ____

NOW TRY THIS!

- **Draw ship M that is NW of ship H, and E of ship D.**

Teachers' note At the start of the lesson, introduce the eight compass points (see page 7). Ensure the children understand that the grid lines upon which each ship sits show the eight compass directions.

100% New Developing Mathematics
Understanding Shapes and
Measures: Ages 8–9
© A & C BLACK

• **Cut out the cards and use them to play the game on Zap 'em: 2.**

Zap a counter if it is **NE** of yours	Zap a counter if it is **SW** of yours	Zap a counter if it is **S** of yours	Zap a counter if it is **NW** of yours
Zap a counter if it is **E** of yours	Zap a counter if it is **SE** of yours	Zap a counter if it is **NE** of yours	Zap a counter if it is **S** of yours
Zap a counter if it is **NW** of yours	Zap a counter if it is **E** of yours	Zap a counter if it is **W** of yours	Zap a counter if it is **NE** of yours
Zap a counter if it is **SW** of yours	Zap a counter if it is **SE** of yours	Zap a counter if it is **N** of yours	Zap a counter if it is **SE** of yours
Zap a counter if it is **W** of yours	Zap a counter if it is **N** of yours	Zap a counter if it is **SW** of yours	Zap a counter if it is **NW** of yours

Teachers' note Use this sheet in conjunction with page 29, Zap 'em: 2. The worksheet could be copied onto card and laminated to create a more permanent resource.

**100% New Developing Mathematics
Understanding Shapes and
Measures: Ages 8–9**
© A & C BLACK

Zap 'em: 2

• Play this game with a partner.

You need counters in two colours (eight of each colour)…

…and the cards cut from Zap 'em: 1.

☆ Take turns to place a counter in your colour on the grid until all the circles are covered.

☆ Place the cards face down in a pile.

☆ Now take turns to pick a card. If one of your partner's counters can be reached from one of yours in the direction shown on the card, remove that counter. You can only zap one counter at a time.

☆ The winner is the first player to zap all their partner's counters.

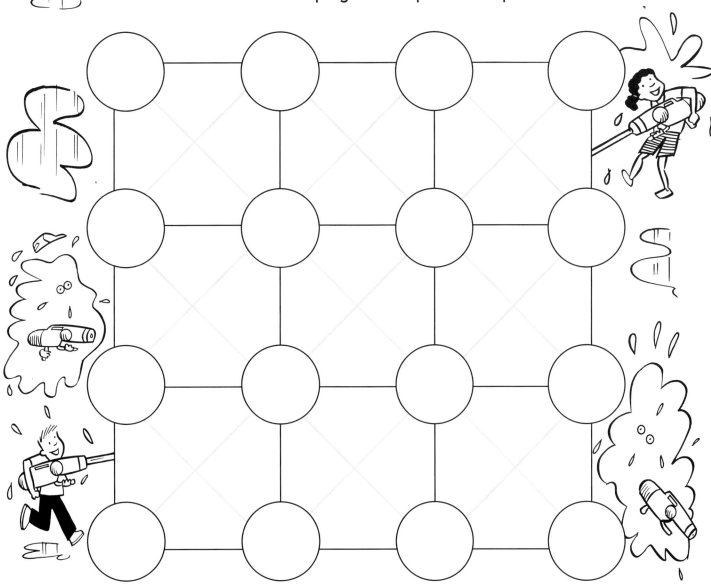

Teachers' note Use this sheet in conjunction with page 28, Zap 'em: 1. The worksheet could be copied onto card and laminated to create a more permanent resource.

100% New Developing Mathematics Understanding Shapes and Measures: Ages 8–9

Counter attack

A counter is placed on a square and then moved.
• Write where the counter ends up each time.

N
NW   NE
W   E
SW   SE
S

	7							
	6							
	5							
	4							
	3							
	2							
	1							

A   B   C   D   E   F   G

1. The counter starts on B4. It moves 1 square NE, then 4 squares SE. It is now on ☐

2. The counter starts on D6. It moves 3 squares SE, then 2 squares SW. It is now on ☐

3. The counter starts on C3. It moves 1 square NW, then 2 squares NE. It is now on ☐

4. The counter starts on F6. It moves 3 squares SW, then 2 squares NE. It is now on ☐

5. The counter starts on B5. It moves 2 squares SE, then 2 squares NW. It is now on ☐

6. The counter starts on C4. It moves 2 squares NW, then 3 squares SE. It is now on ☐

NOW TRY THIS!

• **Make up three puzzles of your own for a partner to solve.**

Teachers' note You may wish to enlarge this sheet to A3. Remind the children of the eight compass directions at the start of the lesson and ensure that the children are confident in locating a square on a grid.

100% New Developing Mathematics
Understanding Shapes and
Measures: Ages 8–9
© A & C BLACK

Cinema seating

• Colour the people's **T-shirts** to match these descriptions.

The man in **C4** has a **green** T-shirt.

The girl in **D3** has a **blue** T-shirt.

The people in **E2** and **F2** have **red** T-shirts.

The boy in **A6** has a **yellow** T-shirt.

The woman in **B3** has an **orange** T-shirt.

The girl in **F6** has a **pink** T-shirt.

The woman in **F5** has a **purple** T-shirt.

The woman in **D5** has a **black** T-shirt.

You need coloured pencils.

NOW TRY THIS!

• Write the positions of the people whose T-shirts you have <u>not</u> coloured. _____

Teachers' note When introducing this activity, remind the children that the letter is given first and then the number to indicate the position of a square in a grid.

100% New Developing Mathematics Understanding Shapes and Measures: Ages 8–9 © A & C BLACK

Hickory, dickory, dock

These clocks show each o'clock time from 1 o'clock to 12 o'clock.

• **Complete the table to show the angles between the hands.**

o'clock	1	2	3	4	5	6	7	8	9	10	11	12
angle			90°									

• **Talk to a partner about any patterns you notice.**

NOW TRY THIS!

This clock shows half past 6.

• **What do you think the angle between the hands is here?** _____

Teachers' note When introducing this activity, begin by exploring the angle between the hands at 3 o'clock, which the children should recognise as a right angle. Then show how the right angle can be split into three equal parts and discuss the angle between the hands at 1 o'clock. Encourage the children to look for patterns in the numbers and to discuss these with a partner.

100% New Developing Mathematics Understanding Shapes and Measures: Ages 8–9 © A & C BLACK

Angelina's angles

Angelina makes a hole in the centre of a circle of card.
She knots a piece of wool, threads it
through the hole and pulls it gently.
She moves her hand to turn the wool
through different angles.

• **Estimate how many degrees she turns the wool through.**

1.
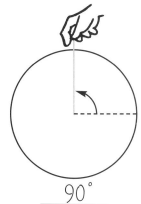
$90°$
_____

2.
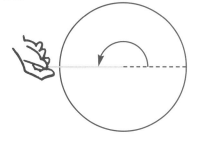
_____

3.
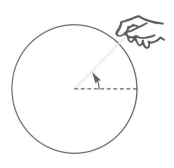
_____

4.
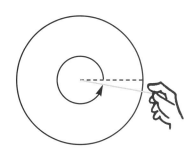
_____

5.
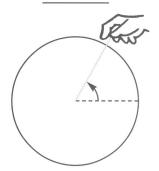
_____

6.
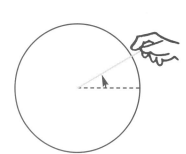
_____

7.
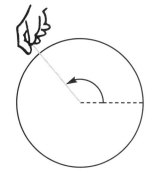
_____

8.
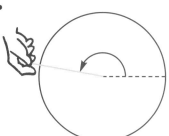
_____

9.
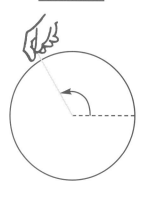
_____

NOW TRY THIS!

• **Write the angles in order of size, starting with the smallest.** _____

Teachers' note Ensure the children know that angles are measured in degrees and that there are 90° in a right angle, 180° in a straight angle and 360° in a full turn. It is useful for children to make their own angle turner following Angelina's approach.

100% New Developing Mathematics
Understanding Shapes and
Measures: Ages 8–9
© A & C BLACK

Safe-breaker

To unlock this safe you must turn each of the five dials through several angles in order.

- Follow the instructions and draw where the arrow should be pointing at the end.

1. Turn 90° clockwise, then 360° anticlockwise, then 180° clockwise.

Start

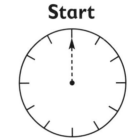

2. Turn 45° clockwise, then 90° anticlockwise, then 180° clockwise.

Start

3. Turn 30° clockwise, then 30° clockwise, then 30° clockwise.

Start

4. Turn 60° clockwise, then 90° anticlockwise, then 30° clockwise.

Start

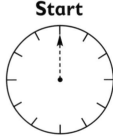

5. Turn 180° clockwise, then 90° anticlockwise, then 30° anticlockwise.

Start

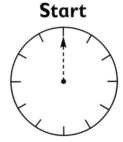

NOW TRY THIS!

- Write your own instructions for five dials on a safe for a partner to solve.

Teachers' note Remind the children of the directions **clockwise** and **anticlockwise**, and demonstrate the sizes of different turns, including 90°, 45°, 30°, 60°, 180° and 360°.

100% New Developing Mathematics
Understanding Shapes and
Measures: Ages 8–9
© A & C BLACK

Maurice faces the first letter of the word. He turns through an angle to face the next letter, and so on.

• **Follow the instructions to spell a word.**

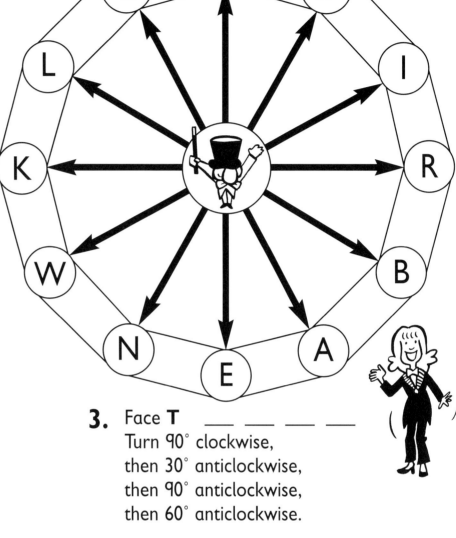

1. Face **W**   A __ __ __
Turn 90° anti-clockwise,
then 60° clockwise,
then 180° clockwise.

2. Face **C** __ __ __
Turn 180° clockwise,
then 60° anticlockwise,
then 60° anticlockwise.

3. Face **T** __ __ __ __ __
Turn 90° clockwise,
then 30° anticlockwise,
then 90° anticlockwise,
then 60° anticlockwise.

4. Face **R** __ __ __ __ __ __
Turn 60° clockwise,
then 30° anticlockwise,
then 360° clockwise,
then 60° anticlockwise,
then 60° anticlockwise.

5. Face **C** __ __ __ __ __
Turn 90° clockwise,
then 30° clockwise,
then 120° anticlockwise,
then 30° anticlockwise,
then 120° anticlockwise.

NOW TRY THIS!

• **Write instructions for some words of your own for a partner to solve.**

Teachers' note Begin the lesson by demonstrating this activity practically (see page 8). Remind the children of the directions **clockwise** and **anticlockwise**, and demonstrate the sizes of different turns, including 90°, 45°, 30°, 60°, 180° and 360°.

**100% New Developing Mathematics
Understanding Shapes and
Measures: Ages 8–9**
© A & C BLACK

Scissor angles

☆ Cut out the cards. Spread them face down on the table.

☆ Each pick a card and compare the angles.

☆ The player with the largest angle keeps that card.
The other players put their cards back.

☆ Mix up the cards and pick again.

☆ Collect the most cards to win the game.

This is a game for 2 to 4 players.

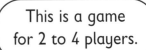

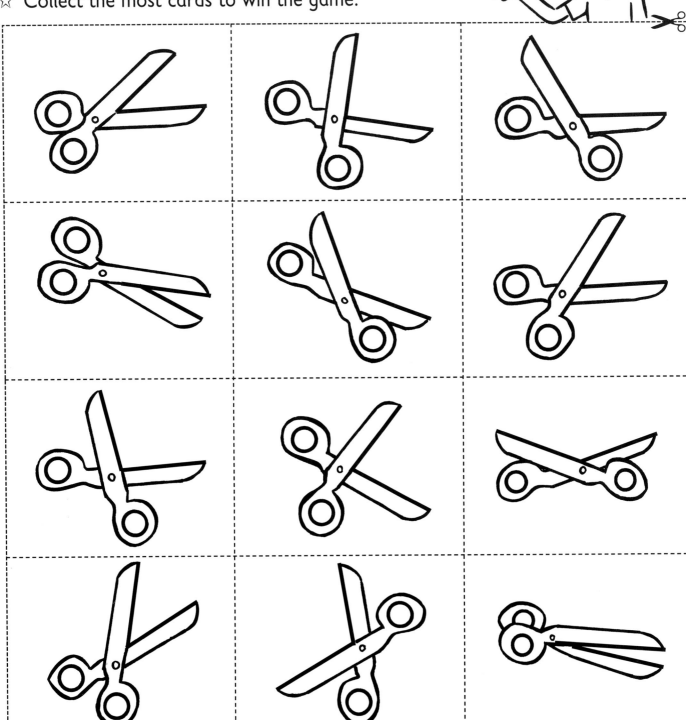

Teachers' note This sheet could be enlarged to A3 size and laminated to create a more permanent classroom resource. Encourage the children to rotate the scissor cards to help them examine and compare the sizes of angles.

100% New Developing Mathematics Understanding Shapes and Measures: Ages 8–9 © A & C BLACK

Angle tangle

- **On each card join three dots to make an angle.**
- **Try to make the angles different sizes.**

One has been done for you.

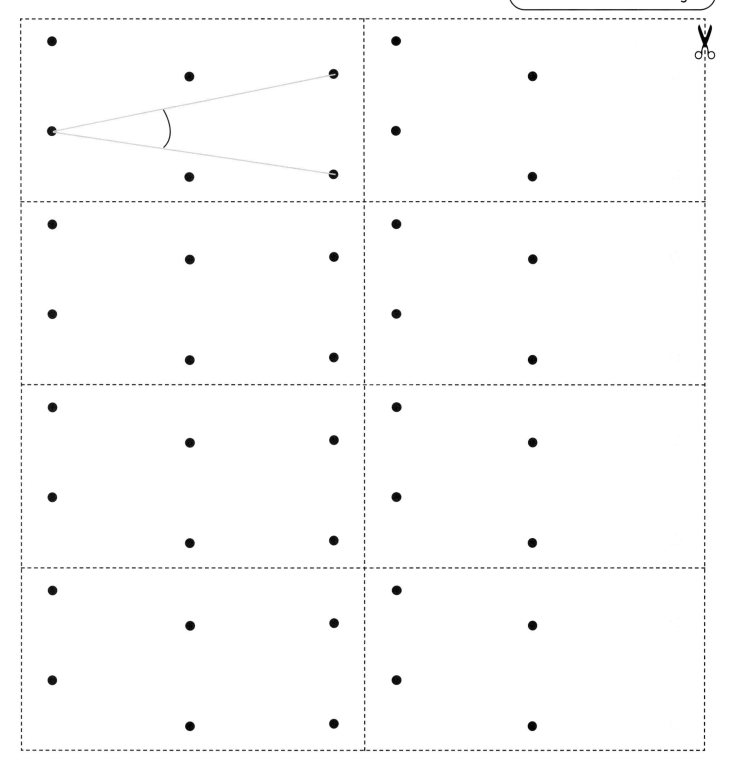

- **Cut out the cards and put the angles in order of size, smallest to largest.**

Teachers' note Encourage the children to begin ordering the angles by seeing which are greater than, equal to or less than a right angle. Draw attention to the fact that angle is the amount of turn from one line to the other, and is not related to line length, area inside the arc or distance between the two end-points of the lines.

100% New Developing Mathematics
Understanding Shapes and
Measures: Ages 8–9
© A & C BLACK

37

That's an order!

- **Put each set of angles in order of size, starting with the smallest.**

1.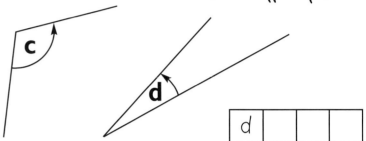

d			

2.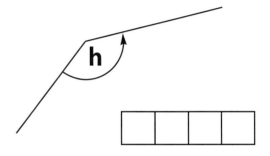

3.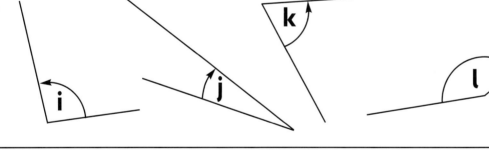

4.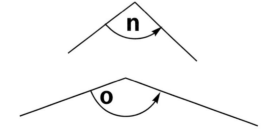

38 **Teachers' note** Encourage the children to begin ordering the angles by seeing which are greater than, equal to or less than a right angle. Draw attention to the fact that angle is the amount of turn from one line to the other, and is not related to line length, area inside the arc or distance between the two end-points of the lines.

100% New Developing Mathematics Understanding Shapes and Measures: Ages 8–9 © A & C BLACK

Measure for measure

Work with a partner or in a small group.

You need some measuring equipment and:

a shoe    a jumper or a sweatshirt

a T-shirt   a trainer or a plimsoll

- **Measure each item and record the measurements below. You should measure to the nearest centimetre and to the nearest gram.**

1.

length [ ]   width [ ]   mass [ ]

area of sole [ ]

2.

length of sleeve [ ]

width of chest [ ]

mass [ ]

3.

length of sleeve [ ]

width of chest [ ]

mass [ ]

4.

length [ ]   width [ ]   mass [ ]

area of sole [ ]

NOW TRY THIS!

- **Do you think the shoe or the trainer has the larger capacity? Or do they have the same capacity?**

Teachers' note Explain that a shop is advertising these items on the Internet and wants to describe them fully. Provide tape measures, rulers and scales, together with squared paper for measuring the area of the soles. Encourage the children to realise the importance of saying what unit is being used.

100% New Developing Mathematics
Understanding Shapes and
Measures: Ages 8–9
© A & C BLACK

Measure together

- **Cut out the cards.**
- **Decide which unit of measurement would be best to use in each answer.**
- **Then try to find the answers to some of the cards.**

Work with a partner.

| mm | cm | m | km | g | kg | ml | l |

What is the mass of an apple?	How much water can a mug hold?	How wide is a CD?
How thin is a matchstick?	What is the distance from London to Edinburgh?	What is the capacity of a teaspoon?
How wide is a computer monitor?	How heavy is a telephone directory?	How much cola is in a large bottle?
How long is an ant?	How far do people run in a marathon?	How heavy is a tin of baked beans?
What is the capacity of a bucket?	How wide is a tennis ball?	How heavy is a football?

Teachers' note The children could write the unit on the back of each card. Discuss other units, such as imperial units, if they arise and at the end of the activity, compare and discuss the children's answers. Where possible provide measuring equipment and some of the items shown or encourage the children to use the Internet or books to find other information.

100% New Developing Mathematics Understanding Shapes and Measures: Ages 8–9
© A & C BLACK

Made to measure

These scarves are different lengths.

• **Write the missing numbers on the scarves.**

Remember:
1m = 100 cm, and
$\frac{1}{10}$ m = 10 cm.

Centi is the Latin word for **hundred**.

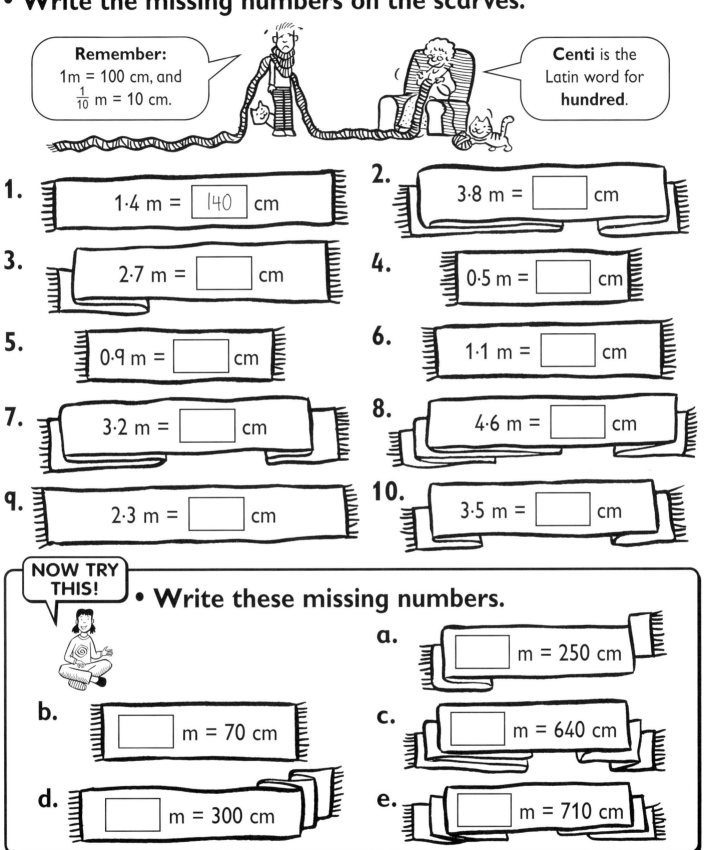

1. 1·4 m = ⟨140⟩ cm

2. 3·8 m = ☐ cm

3. 2·7 m = ☐ cm

4. 0·5 m = ☐ cm

5. 0·9 m = ☐ cm

6. 1·1 m = ☐ cm

7. 3·2 m = ☐ cm

8. 4·6 m = ☐ cm

9. 2·3 m = ☐ cm

10. 3·5 m = ☐ cm

NOW TRY THIS!

• **Write these missing numbers.**

a. ☐ m = 250 cm

b. ☐ m = 70 cm

c. ☐ m = 640 cm

d. ☐ m = 300 cm

e. ☐ m = 710 cm

Teachers' note As the children become more familiar with the relationships between the units they can begin to convert between them, including using decimals. Remind the children that the column after the decimal point tells you how many tenths of a metre (or how many lots of 10 cm) there are.

100% New Developing Mathematics
Understanding Shapes and
Measures: Ages 8–9
© A & C BLACK

Guinea pig food

These sacks of guinea pig food have been weighed.
Pairs of sacks weigh the same.

- **Fill in the missing weights on the sacks.**

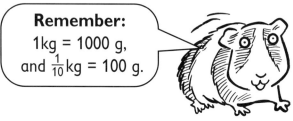

Remember:
1kg = 1000 g,
and $\frac{1}{10}$ kg = 100 g.

Kilo is the
Greek word for
thousand.

1. 2 kg = 2000 g

2. 4·5 kg = ___ g

3. 1·5 kg = ___ g

4. 7·3 kg = ___ g

5. 2·8 kg = ___ g

6. 5·9 kg = ___ g

7. 7 kg = ___ g

8. 0·1 kg = ___ g

NOW TRY THIS!

- **Fill in these missing weights.**

(a) 3600 g = ___ g

(b) 5800 g = ___ g

(c) 700 g = ___ g

Teachers' note As the children become more familiar with the relationships between units they can begin to convert between them, including using decimals. Remind the children that the column after the decimal point tells you how many tenths of a kilogram (or how many lots of 100 g) there are.

**100% New Developing Mathematics
Understanding Shapes and
Measures: Ages 8–9**
© A & C BLACK

Milking Milli

Milli the goat is milked every day.
- **Complete the chart to show how many millilitres of milk she gives each day.**

Milli is the Latin word for **thousand**.

Remember:
one litre is 1000 millilitres;
one-tenth of a litre is 100 ml.

Day	Amount of milk in **litres**	Amount of milk in **millilitres**
Monday	3 l	3000 ml
Tuesday	1·5 l	
Wednesday	2·4 l	
Thursday	1·7 l	
Friday	2·8 l	
Saturday	3·5 l	
Sunday	0·9 l	

NOW TRY THIS!

- **Fill in the amount of milk Milli gives in litres for the following week.**

Day	Amount in litres	Amount in millilitres
Monday	2·4 l	2400 ml
Tuesday		3300 ml
Wednesday		200 ml
Thursday		700 ml
Friday		1100 ml
Saturday		300 ml
Sunday		4400 ml

Teachers' note As the children become more familiar with the relationships between units they can begin to convert between them, including using decimals. Remind the children that the column after the decimal point tells you how many tenths of a litre (or how many lots of 100 ml) there are.

**100% New Developing Mathematics
Understanding Shapes and
Measures: Ages 8–9**
© A & C BLACK

Fi's fruitcake

cocoa

25 g

Fi is making a fruitcake. She keeps adding new ingredients to the scales.

• **Read each new measurement.**

flour

raisins

sultanas

butter

sugar

NOW TRY THIS!

• **How much of each ingredient does Fi put onto the scales?**

cocoa _____ g   flour _____ g   raisins _____ g

sugar _____ g   butter _____ g   sultanas _____ g

Teachers' note Begin the lesson by looking at the scales and determining the value of each interval. Encourage the children to read the scales as accurately as they can. The arrows can be adjusted to provide a range of different scales to read and to provide differentiation.

44

100% New Developing Mathematics
Understanding Shapes and Measures: Ages 8–9
© A & C BLACK

Fill it up!

• Play this game with a partner.

☆ Take turns to roll the dice. Use the key to find out how much water to add to your container.

☆ Use a blue pencil to show each new amount of water.

☆ The winner is the first to **exactly** fill his/her container. (Miss a go if you roll an amount that is more than you need.)

You need a dice and a blue colouring pencil.

⚀	100 ml
⚁	200 ml
⚂	300 ml
⚃	400 ml
⚄	500 ml
⚅	600 ml

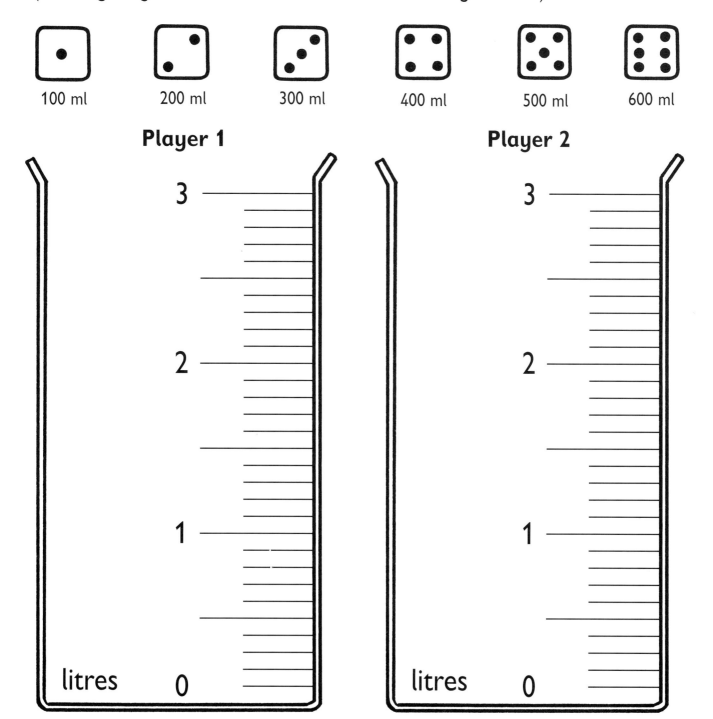

Player 1

3

2

1

litres   0

Player 2

3

2

1

litres   0

Teachers' note Less confident children might benefit from the scales being marked in millilitres rather than litres, i.e. where 500 ml, 1000 ml, 1500 ml, 2000 ml, etc. are marked. Remind the children that there are 1000 ml in one litre and that each mark on this scale represents 100 ml. Ensure the children understand that they must fill their containers to the 3-litre mark.

100% New Developing Mathematics Understanding Shapes and Measures: Ages 8–9 © A & C BLACK

Potion pathways

☆ Read each scale. Tick the answer **yes** or **no** to each question.

☆ Go to **start**. Follow the yes/no routes to the correct pot. Colour it.

☆ Discuss your route with a partner.

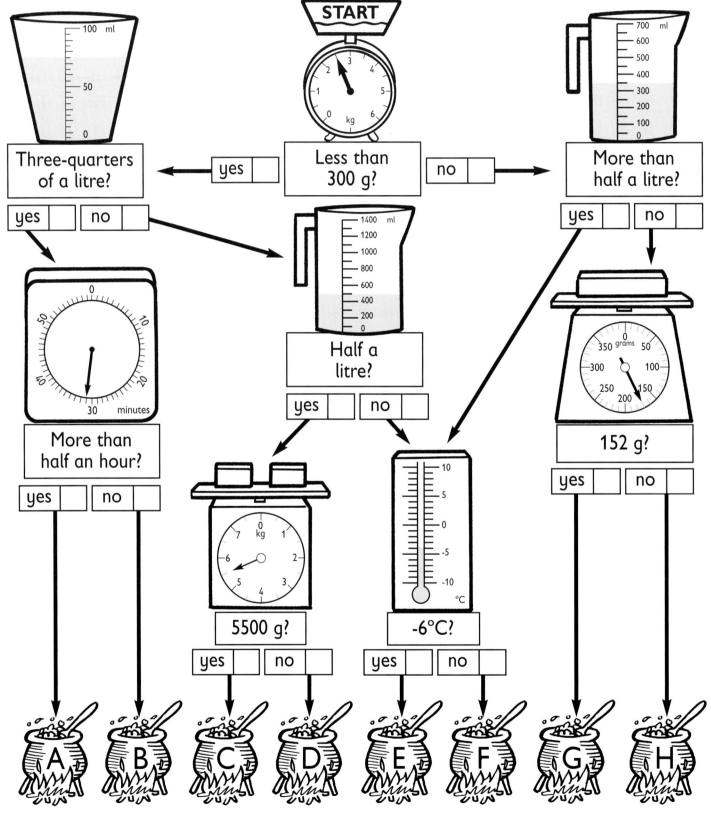

	100 ml
	50
	0

START

3
2 4
1 5
0 6
kg

	700 ml
	600
	500
	400
	300
	200
	100
	0

Three-quarters of a litre?

yes → | **Less than 300 g?** | ← no → | **More than half a litre?** |

yes | no

	1400 ml
	1200
	1000
	800
	600
	400
	200
	0

yes | no

0
50 10
40 20
30 minutes

Half a litre?

0 grams
350 50
300 100
250 150
200

More than half an hour?

yes | no

yes | no

152 g?

0 kg
7 1
6 2
5 3
4

10
5
0
-5
-10
°C

yes | no

5500 g?

-6°C?

yes | no

yes | no

A B C D E F G H

Teachers' note See the notes on pages 9–10 that explain which errors children have made if they choose any of the incorrect pots. Remind the children of the relationships between grams and kilograms and millilitres and litres, and encourage them to say what a half and a quarter of a kilogram and a litre is in grams and millilitres respectively. Encourage discussion with partners.

100% New Developing Mathematics Understanding Shapes and Measures: Ages 8–9
© A & C BLACK

Speedometers

• **Read the scale to work out how fast the car is travelling.**

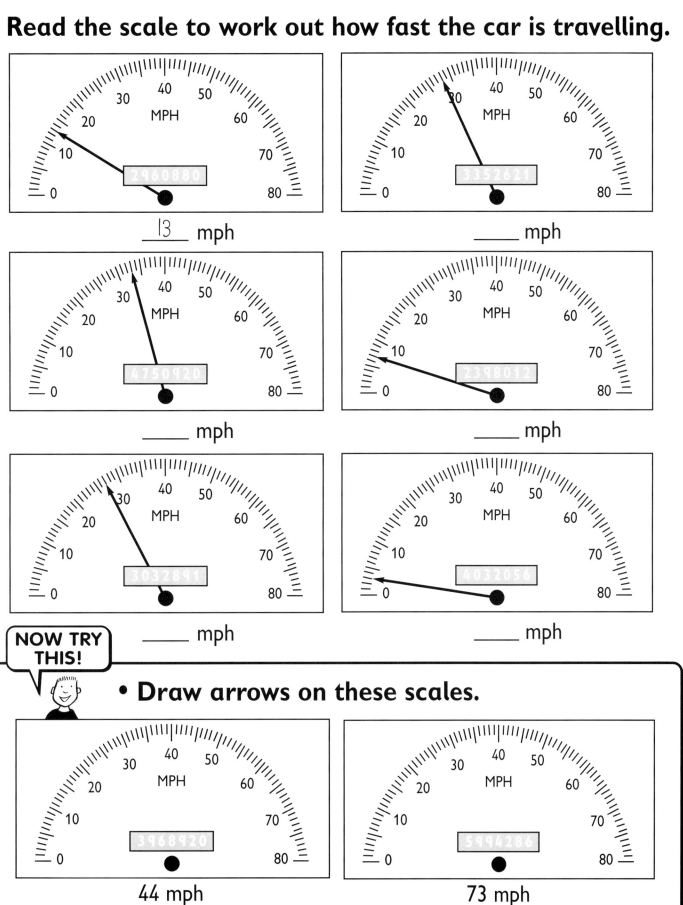

_13_ mph

_____ mph

_____ mph

_____ mph

_____ mph

_____ mph

NOW TRY THIS!

• **Draw arrows on these scales.**

44 mph

73 mph

Teachers' note It is not important for children of this age to fully understand the concept of speed, but this activity focuses on reading scales that children will be familiar with in real life. Explain that 'mph' means 'miles per hour'.

100% New Developing Mathematics
Understanding Shapes and Measures: Ages 8–9
© A & C BLACK

Scale shapes

- ## Match up each letter with a shape in the key below.

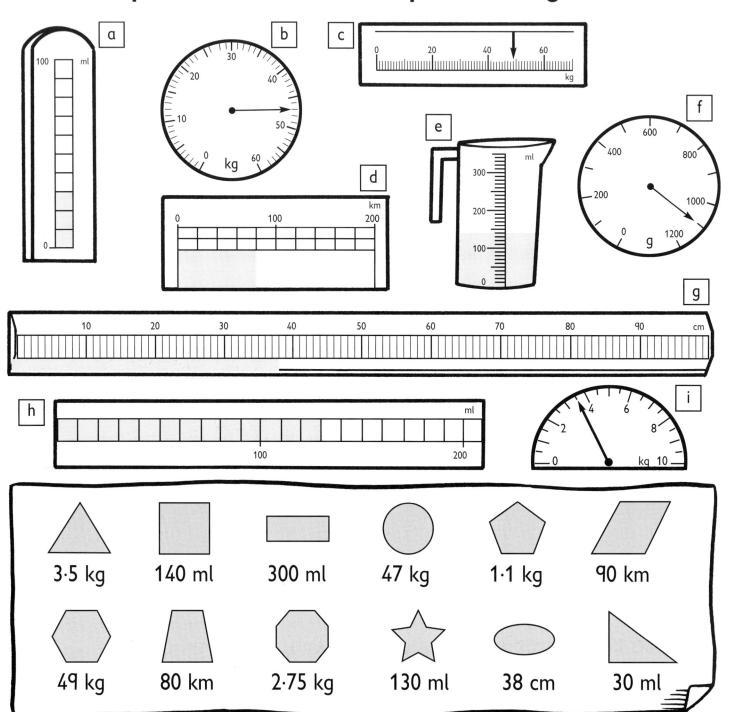

- ## Record your answers here.

a = ◿

Teachers' note Encourage the children to discuss their answers at the end of the lesson and examine scales that have caused difficulties. Draw attention to the fact that some scales are marked in grams but the reading is shown in kilograms, and remind the children of the relationship between these units.

48

100% New Developing Mathematics
Understanding Shapes and
Measures: Ages 8–9
© A & C BLACK

Perimeter puzzles

- **Measure and label the sides of each sticker. Work out the** [perimeter] **of each sticker.**

a

13 cm

This book belongs to

perimeter = _____ cm

b

is Star of the week

perimeter = _____ cm

c

_____'s room

KEEP OUT

perimeter = _____ cm

d

Karate student of the month is

perimeter = _____ cm

- **Solve these perimeter puzzles to find out who each sticker belongs to.**

Write the name on the sticker.

Ali's sticker has a perimeter of 31 cm.

The perimeter of Jo's sticker is 1 cm longer than the perimeter of Ali's sticker.

The badge belonging to Sam has a perimeter that is half the perimeter of Jo's sticker.

The perimeter of Li's sticker is 3 cm longer than the perimeter of Ali's sticker.

Teachers' note Introduce the children to the idea of perimeter as the distance once around the edge of a shape. When completing the sheet, encourage accurate measuring and checking. As an extension, ask the children to draw Fred's sticker – its perimeter is 10 cm longer than Sam's.

100% New Developing Mathematics
Understanding Shapes and
Measures: Ages 8–9
© A & C BLACK

Spot the rectangles

☆ Using a ruler, join four dots to make a rectangle with horizontal and vertical sides.

☆ Measure the sides of the rectangle and record its perimeter in the box below.

☆ Do this for three more rectangles.

The rectangles can overlap.

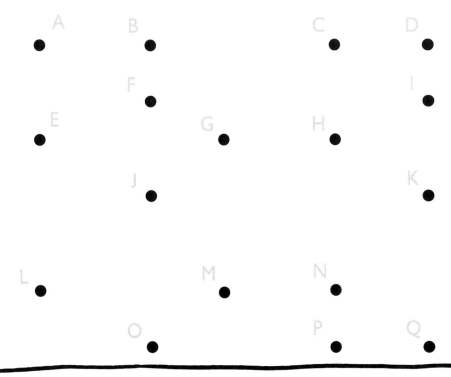

Write the letters of the corners of the rectangles to help you record the perimeters.

NOW TRY THIS!

- **On the back of the sheet, draw three different rectangles, each with a perimeter of 24 cm.**

Teachers' note During the plenary, investigate how many different perimeters the class have found.

50

100% New Developing Mathematics
Understanding Shapes and
Measures: Ages 8–9
© A & C BLACK

Seeing stars

These stars have ten equal sides.

- Measure the length of the side of each star and find its perimeter.

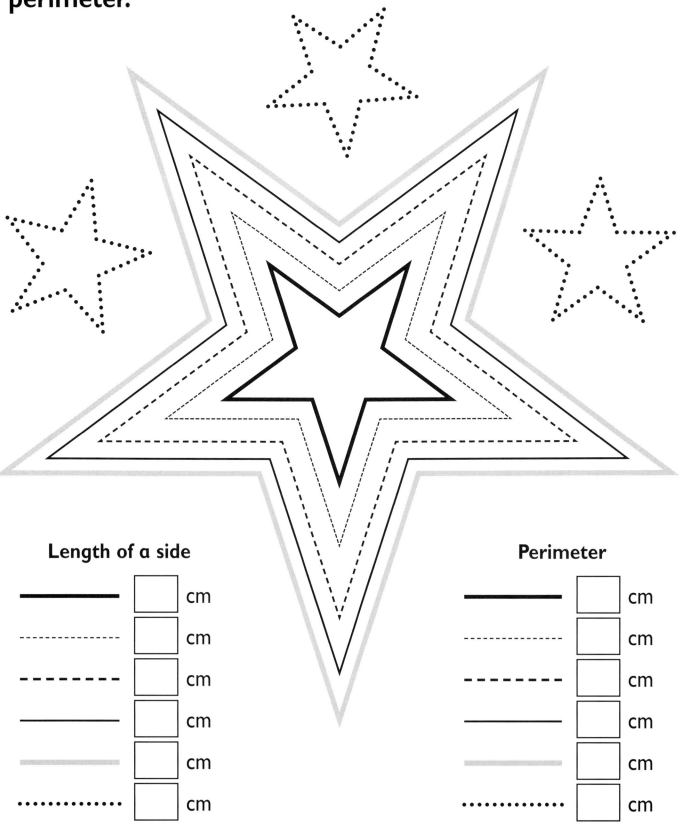

Length of a side		Perimeter	
——————	☐ cm	——————	☐ cm
- - - - - - - -	☐ cm	- - - - - - - -	☐ cm
– – – – –	☐ cm	– – – – –	☐ cm
——————	☐ cm	——————	☐ cm
——————	☐ cm	——————	☐ cm
••••••••••	☐ cm	••••••••••	☐ cm

Teachers' note Encourage the children to measure as accurately as they can, giving measurements to the nearest half-centimetre. During the plenary, discuss how measures such as $2\frac{1}{2}$ cm can be written as 2·5 cm and draw attention to patterns between a decimal and ten times that decimal, for example 2·5 cm and 25 cm.

**100% New Developing Mathematics
Understanding Shapes and
Measures: Ages 8–9**
© A & C BLACK

51

Area llamas

- **Find the** `area` **of each llama.**

One has been done for you.

a

17 cm²

b

c

d

e

f

NOW TRY THIS!

- **On squared paper, draw llamas with areas of:**

    15 cm²   19 cm²   22 cm²

Teachers' note Introduce the children to the idea of area as the number of squares inside an outline and explain that centimetre squares, like the ones above, can be written as 'cm²'. For llama f, ensure the children realise that if a half-square is shaded this is counted as a half, not a whole.

100% New Developing Mathematics
Understanding Shapes and
Measures: Ages 8–9
© A & C BLACK

Mosaic numbers

• **Find the area of each mosaic number by counting the squares.**

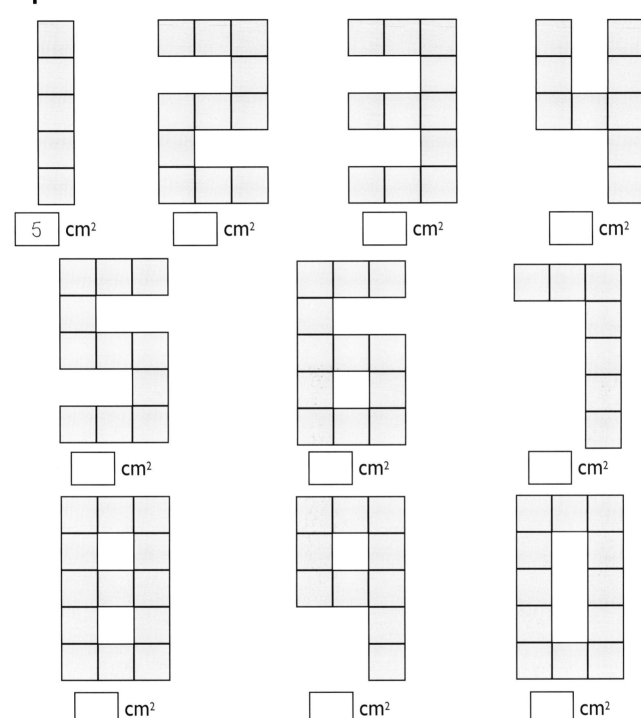

| 5 | cm² | | cm² | | cm² | | cm² |

| | cm² | | cm² | | cm² |

| | cm² | | cm² | | cm² |

NOW TRY THIS!

• **On squared paper, colour your initials.**
• **Then find the area of each mosaic letter.**

Teachers' note Ensure the children understand that area can be found by counting the number of shaded squares making up each number. Explain what is meant by 'initials' to those children attempting the extension activity.

100% New Developing Mathematics
**Understanding Shapes and
Measures: Ages 8–9**
© A & C BLACK

53

Fair and square

1. What do you notice about the perimeter of each grey shape?

_____

2. Now find the area of each grey shape. One has been done for you.

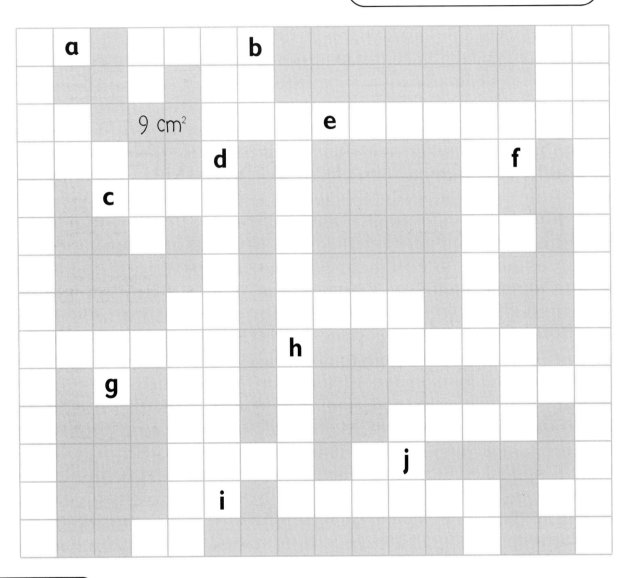

a

b

9 cm²

e

d

f

c

h

g

j

i

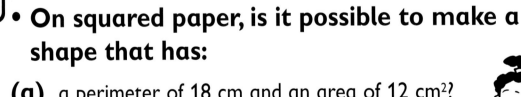

Teachers' note Ensure the children understand that it may not be possible to make all the shapes in the extension activity. Explain also that the shapes must have edges that are horizontal and vertical, and not diagonal.

54

100% New Developing Mathematics
Understanding Shapes and
Measures: Ages 8–9
© A & C BLACK

Time dominoes

- **Cut out the cards.**
- **Play time dominoes with a partner.**

Teachers' note Enlarge the sheet to A3 size and laminate for a more permanent resource. Encourage the children to read the times on the two matching clocks aloud as they lay a domino. As a further activity the children could also pick a domino and work out the time interval between the times shown on the two clocks.

100% New Developing Mathematics Understanding Shapes and Measures: Ages 8–9 © A & C BLACK

55

Time bingo

☆ Tick eight of the times from the list below and draw them onto the blank clocks.

☆ Swap sheets with a partner and check that their clocks match their chosen times.

☆ Now you are ready to play Time bingo!

Your teacher will tell you how.

quarter past one ☐

nine fifty-eight ☐

ten to twelve ☐

two thirty-nine ☐

eleven twenty-two ☐

seven minutes past one ☐

seventeen minutes past four ☐

ten past three ☐

twenty to two ☐

six thirty ☐

eight fifty ☐

twenty-five to seven ☐

ten forty-seven ☐

half past ten ☐

twelve fifteen ☐

six minutes to five ☐

Bingo!

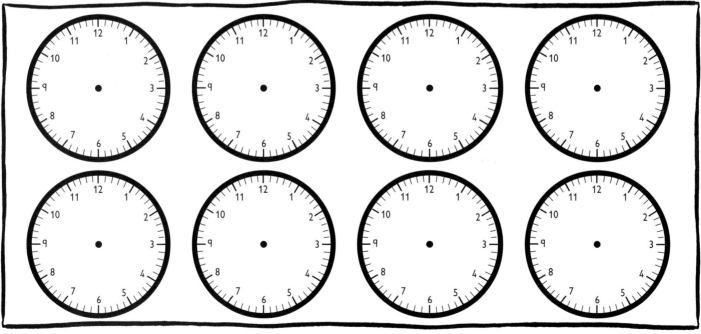

Teachers' note When the times have been drawn on the clocks and checked by a partner, call out times from the list, ideally altering the way they are described, for example 'six thirty' could be read out as 'half past six', or 'eight fifty' as 'ten to nine'.

100% New Developing Mathematics Understanding Shapes and Measures: Ages 8–9
© A & C BLACK

Dan's day

It is Monday.

- Colour the box that shows what Dan is most likely to be doing at these times.

12:15 pm	Going to bed	Getting up
	Eating lunch	In bed

10:10 am	At school	Eating lunch
	Getting up	In bed

1:00 am	Watching TV	At school
	Eating lunch	In bed

4:15 pm	In bed	Getting up
	Eating lunch	Watching TV

3:30 am	Going home	In bed
	Watching TV	Eating lunch

7:30 am	Going to bed	Getting up
	Eating lunch	At school

1:00 pm	At school	Getting up
	Eating breakfast	In bed

NOW TRY THIS!

- Choose any six am and pm times.
- Write what you are usually doing at those times on a weekday.

Teachers' note It is important that children are able to interpret 'am' and 'pm' times, and are not just taught that 'am' represents the hours between midnight and midday and 'pm' the hours between midday and midnight. Encourage the children to talk about the activities they might be doing at different times of the day.

100% New Developing Mathematics Understanding Shapes and Measures: Ages 8–9 © A & C BLACK

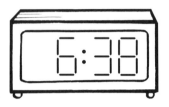

What time would it be 30 minutes later?

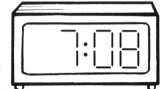

What time would it be 15 minutes later?

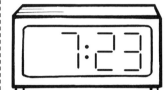

What time would it be $\frac{1}{2}$ an hour earlier?

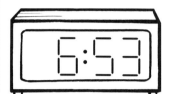

What time would it be 8 minutes later?

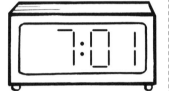

What time would it be $1\frac{1}{2}$ hours earlier?

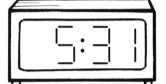

What time would it be 16 minutes later?

What time would it be $\frac{3}{4}$ of an hour earlier?

What time would it be 20 minutes earlier?

What time would it be 40 minutes later?

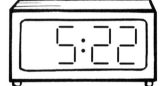

What time would it be $1\frac{1}{4}$ hours later?

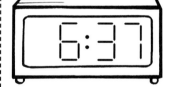

What time would it be $\frac{1}{4}$ of an hour earlier?

What time would it be 5 minutes later?

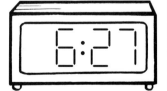

What time would it be 30 minutes earlier?

What time would it be 3 minutes later?

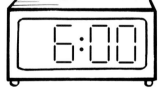

What time would it be 40 minutes later?

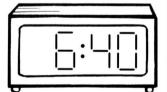

What time would it be 2 minutes earlier?

Teachers' note The loop cards can be given to a large group of children, each with a card (two sets could be used to make 32). Choose a child to say the time and read the question. The first child to stand up with the correct card reads out the time and the new question. The cards can also be used as an individual or pair activity where the children place them correctly in a loop.

100% New Developing Mathematics
Understanding Shapes and
Measures: Ages 8–9
© A & C BLACK

Loopy time intervals: 2

What time
would it be
$\frac{1}{2}$ an hour later?

What time
would it be
10 minutes earlier?

What time
would it be
7 hours earlier?

What time
would it be
20 minutes later?

What time
would it be $\frac{3}{4}$ of
an hour earlier?

What time
would it be
25 minutes earlier?

What time
would it be
6 hours earlier?

What time
would it be
50 minutes later?

What time would
it be 40 minutes
earlier?

What time
would it be
55 minutes later?

What time would
it be $\frac{1}{4}$ of an
hour later?

What time
would it be
5 minutes later?

What time would
it be 45 minutes
earlier?

What time
would it be
8 hours later?

What time
would it be
50 minutes later?

What time
would it be
8 hours earlier?

Teachers' note The loop cards can be given to a large group of children, each with a card (two sets could be used to make 32). Choose a child to say the time and read the question. The first child to stand up with the correct card reads out the time and the new question. The cards can also be used as an individual or pair activity where the children place them correctly in a loop.

**100% New Developing Mathematics
Understanding Shapes and
Measures: Ages 8–9
© A & C BLACK**

Poorly pets

• **Draw the hands on the clock to show the time that each pet should take its next pill.**

1.
It is now

8:53

Take next
pill in
4 hours.

2.
It is now

4:54

Take next
pill in
$\frac{1}{2}$ an hour.

3.
It is now

9:48

Take next
pill in
6 hours.

4.
It is now

2:21

Take next
pill in
45 minutes.

5.
It is now

10:07

Take next
pill in
$2\frac{1}{4}$ hours.

6.
It is now

12:56

Take next
pill in
35 minutes.

NOW TRY THIS!

• **Write the time of this pet's next pill in digital form.**

It is now

8:23

Take next pill in
55 minutes.

:

Teachers' note Provide the children with analogue clocks with moveable, geared hands to help them work out the new times.

100% New Developing Mathematics
Understanding Shapes and
Measures: Ages 8–9
© A & C BLACK

What's the difference?

• **Write how many minutes are between each pair of times.**

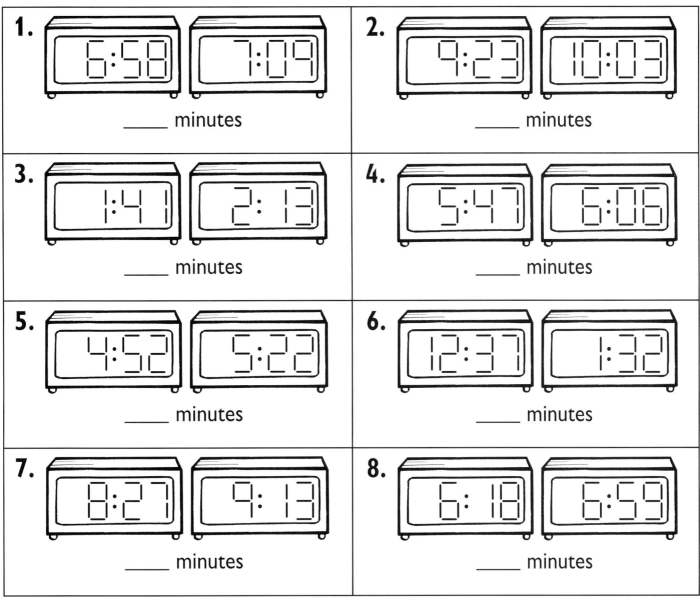

1. 6:58   7:09
    _____ minutes

2. 9:23   10:03
    _____ minutes

3. 1:41   2:13
    _____ minutes

4. 5:47   6:06
    _____ minutes

5. 4:52   5:22
    _____ minutes

6. 12:37   1:32
    _____ minutes

7. 8:27   9:13
    _____ minutes

8. 6:18   6:59
    _____ minutes

NOW TRY THIS!

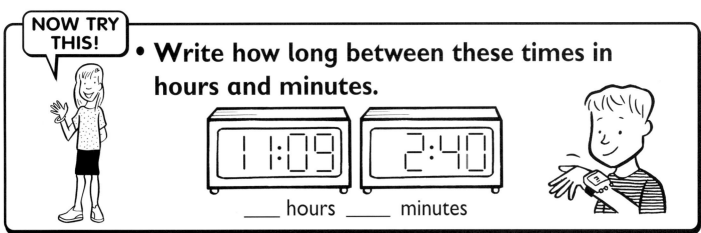

• **Write how long between these times in hours and minutes.**

11:09   2:40

____ hours _____ minutes

Teachers' note Provide the children with analogue clocks, with moveable, geared hands to help them find the time differences. Encourage them to find the hour time between the two given times and to see how many minutes before this hour the first clock shows and then how many minutes after the hour the second clock shows. Then they can add the two numbers of minutes.

100% New Developing Mathematics
Understanding Shapes and
Measures: Ages 8–9
© A & C BLACK

The number 56 bus

- **This is part of a** timetable **for the number 56 bus from Mathschester to Addingham.**

Monday to Friday

Mathschester Bus Station 8:20	8:35	8:50	9:05	9:20	9:35
City Hospital 8:30	8:45	9:00	9:15	9:30	9:45
Football Stadium 8:40	8:55	9:10	9:25	9:40	9:55
Pyramid Shopping Centre 8:50	9:05	9:20	9:35	9:50	10:05
Oval Library 8:55	9:10	9:25	9:40	9:55	10:10
Oval Town Centre 8:59	9:14	9:29	9:44	9:59	10:14
Little Oval 9:09	9:24	9:39	9:54	10:09	10:24
Swimming Pool 9:19	9:34	9:49	10:04	10:19	10:34
Addingham Bus Station 9:32	9:47	10:02	10:17	10:32	10:47

1. How long does it take to get from:

   (a) Mathschester Bus Station to City Hospital? _____ minutes

   (b) Mathschester Bus Station to Pyramid Shopping Centre? _____ minutes

   (c) the Football Stadium to Oval Library? _____ minutes

   (d) Oval Town Centre to Little Oval? _____ minutes

   (e) Little Oval to the Swimming Pool? _____ minutes

   (f) the Swimming Pool to Addingham Bus Station? _____ minutes

2. Joe left Oval Library at 9:40. What time did he get to Little Oval? _____

3. Li left City Hospital at 9:30. What time did she get to Oval Town Centre? _____

NOW TRY THIS!

- **Make up three timetable questions for a partner to solve.**

Teachers' note Provide oral questions to give the children further practice of this kind of activity. Using this or other timetables, encourage the children to work out time intervals and to interpret the timetables.

100% New Developing Mathematics Understanding Shapes and Measures: Ages 8–9 © A & C BLACK

Answers

p 16

p 17

Now try this!

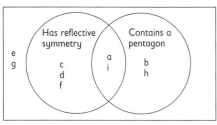

p 19

Presents b, c, f, g and i should be coloured.

Now try this!

1. h   **2.** d   **3.** j   **4.** i   **5.** c   **6.** f

p 20

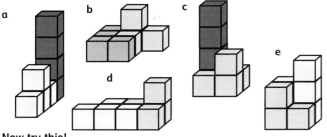

Now try this!

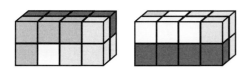

p 25

1. b   **2.** c   **3.** b

p 27

1. SE   **2.** E   **3.** S   **4.** SW   **5.** N   **6.** SW
7. N   **8.** SW   **9.** W   **10.** NE   **11.** S   **12.** NW

p 30

1. G1   **2.** E1   **3.** D6   **4.** E5   **5.** B5   **6.** D3

p 31

Now try this!

A3, B1, B2, B5, C1, C3, C5, C6, D1, D4, E3, E4, E5, F1

p 32

o'clock	1	2	3	4	5	6	7	8	9	10	11	12
angle	30°	60°	90°	120°	150°	180°	210°	240°	270°	300°	330°	360°

Now try this!

15°

p 33

Approximate answers:

1. 90°   **2.** 180°   **3.** 45°   **4.** 350°   **5.** 60°
6. 30°   **7.** 130°   **8.** 170°   **9.** 120°

Now try this!

30°, 45°, 60°, 90°, 120°, 130°, 170°, 180°, 350°

p 34

1.

2.

3.

4.

5.

p 35

1. WAND   **2.** CARD   **3.** TRICK   **4.** RABBIT   **5.** CIRCLE

p 38

1. d, a, b, c   **2.** g, e, f, h   **3.** j, k, i, l   **4.** p, m, n, o

p 41

1. 140 cm   **2.** 380 cm
3. 270 cm   **4.** 50 cm
5. 90 cm   **6.** 110 cm
7. 320 cm   **8.** 460 cm
9. 230 cm   **10.** 350 cm

Now try this!

(a) 2·5 m   **(b)** 0·7 m   **(c)** 6·4 m   **(d)** 3 m   **(e)** 7·1 m

p 42

1. 2000 g   **2.** 4500 g   **3.** 1500 g   **4.** 7300 g
5. 2800 g   **6.** 5900 g   **7.** 7000 g   **8.** 100 g

Now try this!

(a) 3·6 kg   **(b)** 5·8 kg   **(c)** 0·7 kg

p 43

3000 ml   1500 ml   2400 ml   1700 ml   2800 ml   3500 ml   900 ml

Now try this!

2·4 l   3·3 l   0·2 l   0·7 l   1·1 l   0·3 l   4·4 l

p 44

25 g ➤ 150 g ➤ 250 g ➤ 325 g ➤ 475 g ➤ 650 g

Now try this!

cocoa 25 g   flour 125 g   raisins 100 g
sugar 75 g   butter 150 g   sultanas 175 g

p 46
Pot H should be coloured.

p 47
1. 13 mph   **2.** 28 mph   **3.** 33 mph   **4.** 7 mph
5. 27 mph   **6.** 3 mph

p 48

a   b   c   d

e   f   g   h   i

p 49
a sides 13 cm and 4 cm; perimeter 34 cm; sticker belongs to Li
b sides 2·5 cm and 5·5 cm; perimeter 16 cm; sticker belongs to Sam
c sides 8 cm and 7·5 cm; perimeter 31 cm; sticker belongs to Ali
d sides 7·5 cm and 8·5 cm; perimeter 32 cm; sticker belongs to Jo

p 51
Thick black line star: 2·5 cm each side, perimeter 25 cm
Thin dashed line star: 3·5 cm each side, perimeter 35 cm
Thick dashed line star: 5 cm each side, perimeter 50 cm
Black line star: 6 cm each side, perimeter 60 cm
Grey star: 7 cm each side, perimeter 70 cm
Dotted stars: 1·5 cm each side, perimeter 15 cm

p 52
a 17 cm^2 **b** 19 cm^2
c 20 cm^2 **d** 15 cm^2
e 17 cm^2 **f** 19 cm^2

p 53
Numeral 1 5 cm^2 **2** 11 cm^2 **3** 11 cm^2 **4** 9 cm^2 **5** 11 cm^2
6 12 cm^2 **7** 7 cm^2 **8** 13 cm^2 **9** 10 cm^2 **10** 12 cm^2

p 54
1. They all have a perimeter of 18 cm^2.

2. a 9 cm^2 **b** 14 cm^2
   c 11 cm^2 **d** 8 cm^2
   e 17 cm^2 **f** 9 cm^2
   g 13 cm^2 **h** 10 cm^2
   i 8 cm^2 **j** 8 cm^2

Now try this!
All are possible:

Perimeter 18 cm, area 12 cm^2

Perimeter 18 cm, area 15 cm^2

Perimeter 18 cm, area 16 cm^2

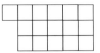

p 57
These are the most likely answers:

Eating lunch
At school
In bed
Watching TV
In bed
Getting up
At school

p 60
1. 12:53   **2.** 5:24
3. 3:48   **4.** 3:06
5. 12:22   **6.** 1:31

Now try this!
9:18

p 61
1. 11 minutes   **2.** 40 minutes
3. 32 minutes   **4.** 19 minutes
5. 30 minutes   **6.** 55 minutes
7. 46 minutes   **8.** 41 minutes

Now try this!
3 hours 31 minutes

p 62
1. (a) 10 minutes   **(b)** 30 minutes
   (c) 15 minutes   **(d)** 10 minutes
   (e) 10 minutes   **(f)** 13 minutes
2. 9:54
3. 9:59